The JavaScript PocketGuide

Lenny**Burdette**

W0009619

Ginormous knowledge, pocket-sized.

**Peachpit
Press**

The JavaScript Pocket Guide
Lenny Burdette

Peachpit Press
1249 Eighth Street
Berkeley, CA 94710
510/524-2178
510/524-2221 (fax)

Find us on the Web at: www.peachpit.com
To report errors, please send a note to: errata@peachpit.com

Peachpit Press is a division of Pearson Education.
Copyright © 2010 by Lenny Burdette

Executive Editor: Clifford Colby
Editor: Kim Wimpsett
Production Editor: Cory Borman
Compositor: David Van Ness
Indexer: Jack Lewis
Cover Design: Peachpit Press
Cover Illustrator: Lenny Burdette and Aren Howell
Interior Design: Peachpit Press

ISBN-13:   978-0-321-70095-7
ISBN-10:   0-321-70095-3

9 8 7 6 5 4 3 2 1

Printed and bound in the United States of America

To my mom and dad

About the Author

In the seventh grade, Lenny Burdette checked out the book *Teach Yourself HTML in 24 Hours* from the public library, and the rest, as they say, is history. Since graduating from UCLA, Burdette has worked at Schematic in Los Angeles, California, where he is the reigning Guitar Hero champion. Schematic (*http://www.schematic.com*) is a digital marking agency that has given him opportunities to develop JavaScript for Web sites, e-commerce platforms, TV, and mobile.

Acknowledgments

I'd first like to thank Cliff Colby and Bruce Hyslop for the opportunity to write this book as well the faith that I could. Huge thanks go to editor Kim Wimpsett and the rest of the team at Peachpit Press for making the process go more smoothly than I ever imagined it would.

Adam Luikart's feedback and sharp eye were invaluable throughout the writing process. All of my colleagues at Schematic, especially Richard Herrera and the rest of IEG, are a wealth of inspiration and support. Additionally, Nick Rodriguez and Dan Duvall were incredibly gracious to look over my work; I own them both many beers.

I wouldn't be where I am without all the teachers I've had through my life, from Mrs. Rhea all the way to Casey Reas. Much thanks to Mr. Fairchild especially, since it was in his class where my love of the Web began.

And of course, thanks to my family, Mom, Dad, Julie, and Rachel, for their love and support.

Contents

Introduction

Between e-mail applications, social networking sites, online word processors, and mobile Web browsers, the Internet is becoming more useful and more powerful every day. A lot of that power comes from JavaScript, a quirky little language available on nearly every computer in the world through browsers such as Internet Explorer, Firefox, Safari, Opera, and Chrome. Brendan Eich created the language for the Netscape browser in 1995, naming it after Java even though the languages have only superficial similarities. Its formal name is ECMAScript, governed by the European Computer Manufacturers Association (ECMA), which published the fifth edition of the language in December 2009.

JavaScript is a *scripting language*, meaning it gives you the ability to control an environment with code. In the case of JavaScript, the environment is usually a Web page in a browser, where you can react to the mouse and keyboard, create and animate elements on the page, communicate with servers, and much more.

Why JavaScript Is Cool

The following are the reasons why JavaScript is cool—or at least why *I* think it's cool:

- **Low barrier to entry.** Anyone can start writing and testing JavaScript code with software they already have on their computer.

- **Easy of deployment.** All you need to include JavaScript on your Web site is a server to store the code files and the <script> tag.

- **Small language, big power.** The language has a relatively small number of features, but its flexibility and expressiveness lets you accomplish a great deal.

- **The quirkiness.** JavaScript has a lot of little oddities and flaws that I find fascinating. It seems like I learn a new nuance to the language every week. Some nuances are even useful!

- **The language of the moment.** JavaScript is becoming more important and more powerful as our lives are increasingly impacted by the Internet.

- **The community.** I'm continually amazed at the brilliance and ingenuity of the JavaScript community, most of whom release their code for anyone to use for free.

Who Should Read This Book

You'll need a solid foundation of HTML and CSS because there's little room to explain either of those languages in this book. Ideally, you've seen JavaScript before; maybe you've even copied some code from an online tutorial into your blog. If you're coming from a different programming background, I'll briefly touch on the factors that make JavaScript fairly unique among popular languages today.

What You Need to Follow Along

You need a text editor to write JavaScript files, ideally one with syntax highlighting such as Notepad2 for Windows or TextWrangler for Mac OS X (both free). Also, because of security restrictions in Web browsers, you will need a server to try the Ajax examples, either running on your own computer or running on the Web. XAMPP (*http://www.apachefriends.org/en/xampp.html*) is a good program to get a server running quickly on your own computer.

What's in This Book

The first half of this book (Chapters 1–8) begins with some basics followed by explanations of the fundamental parts of the language. You won't learn too many practical uses of JavaScript until the second half (Chapters 9–17), which covers programming Web pages and contains in-depth tutorials for a variety of tasks. Throughout the chapters and code examples, I emphasize the important concepts more than the minute details, but you'll also be able to take much of this code and use it in your own sites right away.

What's Not in This Book

I'm not trying to cover everything about JavaScript. Some parts of the scripting language are problematic and not worth using. Other parts are used too infrequently to mention; if I haven't used it in my own code in the last few years, I'm not including it here. And many parts are just too new to be useful, because browser makers still have yet to implement them (which is a shame because there's some exciting stuff just around the corner).

Also, I'm not diving into performance and optimization. JavaScript is tricky enough to learn without getting into the obscure tricks that make your code slightly faster. Once you get the hang of it, though, plenty of books and online resources are available to help you write efficient JavaScript code.

You can find all of the code examples from the tutorial chapters of this book, as well as a few bonus chapters, on its companion Web site *http://www.peachpit.com/javascriptpocketguide*.

Resources

While you're online, here are two of my favorite JavaScript resources on the Web for further reading:

YUI Theater. I especially like Douglas Crockford's presentations about the language and its history. *http://developer.yahoo.com/yui/theater/*

Mozilla Developer Center. This site covers more than just JavaScript, but it's one of the most comprehensive resources, especially for new language features. *https://developer.mozilla.org/*

Writing JavaScript Code

When learning to write JavaScript, it's easy to make simple mistakes that cause your whole script to fail. Here are some tips and guidelines to keep you from pulling your hair out.

Case Sensitivity

When you name a variable or function, pay attention to your uppercase and lowercase letters. JavaScript is not that same thing as javascript. Also, you must refer to built-in objects with the proper casing. Math and Date start with uppercase letters, but not window and document. Most built-in methods are combined words by capitalizing all but the first, such as getElementById (often referred to as *camelCase*).

Comments

Comments are an important part of the coding process even though they don't actually do anything. They are helpful hints for other people who might read your code. More often, they remind me of why I wrote that weird piece of code yesterday.

Single-line comments look like this:

```
// This is a single-line comment
```

```
return true; // Comment after code
```

Multiline comments look like this:

```
/* This comment can wrap
into the next line */
```

Semicolons

JavaScript statements should end with semicolon like sentences end with a period. Technically they are optional, but that's only because JavaScript interpreters add them automatically at the end of most lines. It's best to get into the habit of adding the semicolons yourself because there can be strange side effects when you let the interpreter do it for you. All of the examples in this book strive to demonstrate proper semicolon usage.

Whitespace and New Lines

Most whitespace such as spaces, tabs, and empty lines is ignored in JavaScript and usually just aids readability. In fact, on large-scale production code, all nonessential whitespace is usually stripped out so that script files download quicker. In my examples, I'll try to demonstrate how best to use whitespace for readability.

Reserved Words

JavaScript reserves certain words for specific uses, so be careful to avoid the following unless you mean to use them:

break	for	throw
case	function	try
catch	if	typeof
continue	in	var
default	instanceof	void
delete	new	while
do	return	with
else	switch	
finally	this	

You should also avoid these words because they may be used in future versions of JavaScript:

abstract	final	protected
boolean	float	public
byte	goto	short
char	implements	static
class	import	super
const	int	synchronized
debugger	interface	throws
double	long	transient
enum	native	volatile
export	package	
extends	private	

These words refer to useful objects in the language and Web pages, so be careful not to redefine them with your own values:

arguments	EvalError	parseInt
Array	Function	RangeError
Boolean	Infinity	ReferenceError
Date	isFinite	RegExp
decodeURI	isNaN	String
decodeURIComponent	Math	SyntaxError
encodeURI	NaN	TypeError
Error	Number	undefined
escape	Object	unescape
eval	parseFloat	URIError

Balanced Brackets and Quotes

It is easy to make mistakes when it comes to punctuation. Remember that every time you open a bracket, such as [, (, or {, or a quote mark, such as ' or ", you must close it in the correct order. It can be trickier than you think.

```
(function() {
    alert([1,2,3].join(","));
})();
```

Firebug

My favorite way to explore JavaScript is to use the Firebug extension for Mozilla Firefox, because its Console tab gives you a way to run a snippet of JavaScript and quickly see the result. I'll use Firebug to demonstrate how JavaScript works throughout most of the book, so to follow along with the examples, you'll want to download and install it (*http://getfirebug.com*).

After you install Firebug, load up a Web page and click the Firebug icon (**Figure I.1**) in the lower-right corner of Firefox. You type single-line JavaScript statements into the bottom of the Console tab and hit Enter/Return to execute the code. To type multiple lines at once, expand the text box by clicking the arrow on the right (**Figure I.2**). In this book, the regular code in the examples demonstrates what you enter into Firebug, and the highlighted code gives you an example of the result. (The function console.log() is another way to print output to the console; I'll cover functions in Chapter 5.)

Figure I.1

Firebug open in Firefox.

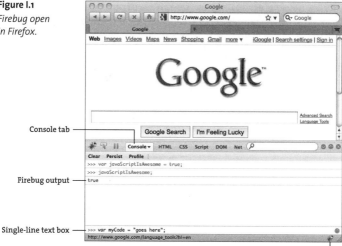

Console tab

Firebug output

Single-line text box

Firebug icon

Figure I.2

The multiline text box in Firebug.

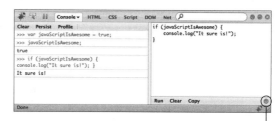

Button to switch between single-line
and multiline text box

tip   You may need to "enable" the console (**Figure I.3**) and refresh the Web page. The console doesn't work unless you've visited a page first, so I usually load Google.com.

Figure I.3
Enabling the console.

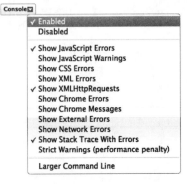

Most modern browsers—including Apple's Safari, Google's Chrome, Opera Software's Opera, and Microsoft's Internet Explorer 8—have a built-in JavaScript console if you prefer to use a browser other than Firefox. I find Firebug's output to be the most useful, however, so the example output printed in this book may not match what you see if you use another browser.

Now that you have the Firebug extension for Firefox set up (or are using another browser), you're ready to write some JavaScript code.

JavaScript Basics

A lot of people learn JavaScript by copying and pasting code they find on the Web without really understanding it. In this book, you'll start from the very beginning.

A language is a system for organizing and transmitting meaning through symbols. A computer language uses symbols you can type with any average keyboard to organize and transmit instructions to hardware and software.

The JavaScript language doesn't have a large number of symbols. Instead, it's very flexible in how you can combine those symbols. That flexibility allows you to produce expressive and powerful code, but it also creates the potential for ambiguity and confusion. Symbols in the language combine to create *syntax*, which acts as the structure or grammar of the language. Values, variables, and functions are the subjects and actions.

Once you get the hang of the symbols and syntax, learning JavaScript is a matter of understanding the various data types you can use. JavaScript includes a few built-in data types, most of which I'll cover in Chapters 2 through 7. If you're using JavaScript in a browser, you have access to many more data types, which will be the focus of Chapters 9, 10, and 11.

Expressions and Statements

Expressions are phrases that produce a value. JavaScript code is made up mostly of expressions in various forms.

Statements are phrases that don't produce a value but instead have some sort of side effect. Examples of side effects include storing variables in memory and jumping to a different part of the script. Statements often combine keywords such as var, if, or while with one or more expressions so that the side effects have values to work with.

Firebug makes it easy to differentiate between expressions and statements. When you enter an expression, it outputs the resulting value:

```
1 + 2;
3
```

When you enter a statement, Firebug doesn't show you any output, even if the statement includes some expressions. That's why I have to use console.log() in some of my examples. This if statement doesn't produce a value. Instead, it controls whether to evaluate the *block* (the code in curly braces).

```
if (true) {
    console.log("expression");
}
```

note   Enter this code example into the multiline text box in Firefox, because hitting Enter/Return in the single-line text box will execute the incomplete code and cause an error.

Variables and Data

Variables store a value you can refer to later in the script. Variable names can be nearly any valid identifier. A JavaScript *identifier* is a word that contains only letters, numbers, $, and _, and that doesn't start with a number.

Variables are a great demonstration of how statements and expressions can be combined. You use a *variable declaration* statement to create a variable.

```
var myVariable;
```

If you already have a variable, you can use a *variable assignment* expression to assign it a value.

```
myVariable = 42;
42
```

You can combine a variable declaration with an assignment expression.

```
var myVariable = 42;
```

You can also string together several variable declarations with commas. Don't forget the commas, though! Leaving off a comma can have the unintended side effect of declaring a global variable when you don't mean to do that. I'll explain that more in Chapter 5.

```
var variable1 = 4,
    variable2 = 8,
    variable3 = 15;
```

Values

JavaScript has a relatively small number of built-in data types, including these common types:

```
var myNumber = 42;
var myString = "A string of text";
var myBoolean = true;
var myArray = [myNumber, myString, myBoolean];
```

Arrays are ordered lists of values, and you can access a particular value by its *index*, or its position in the list. Indices always start at zero.

```
myArray[0];
42
myArray[2];
true
```

For *primitive* values (Number, String, and Boolean), you can find the data type of the variable with the typeof operator.

```
typeof myNumber;
"number"
typeof myString;
"string"
typeof myBoolean;
"boolean"
typeof myArray;
"object"
```

Whoops! Arrays are not primitive values but examples of *objects*, or collections of values. The quick-and-dirty way of checking whether a variable is an array is to use the instanceof operator.

```
myArray instanceof Array;
true
```

You can also declare a variable without a value, in case you want to assign the value later.

```
var myVariable;
typeof myVariable;
"undefined"
```

And unlike strongly typed languages such as C and Java, you can change the type of data stored on a variable.

```
myVariable = 42;
myVariable = "Now it's a string";
myVariable = true;
```

The null value represents the intentional absence of any other value.

```
myVariable = null;
```

Comparison

Comparison expressions return a Boolean. Booleans are the simplest data type, representing either true or false. There are two comparison operators, equality (==) and identity (===). Don't confuse them with the assignment (=) operator that you've already used to assign values to variables.

```
var myNumber = 42;
42
myNumber == 42; // Does it equal the number 42?
true
myNumber == "42"; // Does it equal the string "42"?
true
myNumber === "42"; // Is it identical to the string "42"?
false
```

The equality operator tries to reconcile different data types, such as converting the string "42" to the number 42, before making the comparison. The identity operator does not do any type coercion. The comparison operators have *not* (!) versions for checking inequality and nonidentity.

```
myNumber != 108;
true
myNumber !== "42";
true
```

Comparing *composite* values such as arrays and objects is different from comparing primitive values such as numbers and strings.

```
var array1 = [1, 2, 3];
var array2 = [1, 2, 3];
array1 == array2;
false
array1 === array2;
false
array1 == array1; // Same object
true
array1 === array1; // Equal and identical
true
```

The comparison operators check whether the values are actually the same object instead of checking to see whether it is composed of all the same values in the same order.

Truthiness and Falsiness

All values in JavaScript have a notion of "truthiness" and "falsiness," meaning they can often be treated as true or false values without actually being Booleans. Here are some examples of truthiness:

```
if (1) {
    console.log(true);
}
if ("Nonempty string") {
    console.log(true);
}
if ([]) { // Empty array; all composite values are truthy
    console.log(true);
}
```

Zero, null, undefined, and empty string values are all "falsey," and every other value is "truthy." Both of these examples output false to the console:

```
if (0) {
    console.log(true);
} else {
    console.log(false);
}

if ("") { // Empty string
    console.log(true);
} else {
    console.log(false);
}
```

Use the identity (===) operator if you need to know that a value is actually true or false.

```
myBoolean === true; true
// Truthy but not true
myBoolean === 1; false
```

Functions and Objects

Primitive data types such as Numbers, Strings, and Booleans are fairly straightforward, but the real power of JavaScript comes from functions and objects.

You can break up your code into logical, reusable chunks by using *functions*. Functions can take input, called *arguments*, and execute differently based on that input. In the following example, name is an argument passed to the sayHello() function:

```javascript
function sayHello(name) {
    console.log("Hello, " + name + "!");
}

sayHello("Lenny");
"Hello Lenny!"
sayHello("Sally");
"Hello Sally!"
```

Functions can also *return* a value. Here's a function that calculates the hypotenuse of a right triangle based on the lengths of the other two sides, using the square root function (Math.sqrt()):

```javascript
function hypontenuse(sideA, sideB) {
    return Math.sqrt(sideA * sideA + sideB * sideB);
}

var sideC = hypotenuse(3, 4);
console.log(sideC); 5
```

In JavaScript, functions are just another data type, so you can assign a function to a variable.

```
var myFunc = function() {
    return 42;
};
typeof myFunc; "function"
myFunc(); 42
```

Functions are also an incredibly useful tool for organizing your code and acting upon values. You'll use them throughout the first few chapters before exploring them in more depth in Chapter 5.

Objects

Objects are so fundamental to JavaScript that it is considered an *object-oriented* language. An *object* is a collection of values called *properties*. You usually access a property of an object with the *dot* (.) operator followed by the name of the property.

```
var myObject = {};
myObject.property = 42;
42
myObject.anotherProperty = "value";
"value"
myObject;
Object property=42 anotherProperty="value"
```

 Clicking an object in the Firebug console takes you to the DOM tab and shows you all the object's properties and values.

You can create any number of objects with any number of properties. Properties can be any value, including other objects and functions.

When a property is function, it's referred to as a *method*. The first several chapters cover many of the methods for built-in data types, after which you'll learn to create your own methods. Together, objects and functions make JavaScript a powerful and flexible language. I'll cover the various uses of objects in Chapter 6.

Loops

Computers are great at doing something over and over, making our human lives easier. Say you wanted to print "I am awesome!" in the console 10 times. Instead of typing console.log("I am awesome!") over and over, you can use a loop.

```
var times = 10;
while (times--) {
    console.log("I am awesome!");
}
```

The while statement tests the expression inside the parentheses for truthiness and executes the code block repeatedly. times-- is shorthand for times = times - 1 (also called the *decrement operator*). When times reaches 0, the expression evaluates to false, and the while loop ends.

Another common loop is the for statement, which takes three expressions separated by semicolons.

```
for (var i = 0; i < 10; i++) {
    console.log("Loop number " + i);
}
```

The first expression, var i = 0, is the *setup*, which runs once. The second, i < 10, is the *test*, which runs each time the loop executes until i is no longer less than 10. The last is the *increment*—in this case, it actually uses the increment (++) operator, which adds 1 to i each time around. You can often use while and for interchangeably.

Make sure that your *test* expressions eventually become "falsey," or the loop will never end:

```javascript
var counter = 0;
while (counter < 10) {
    console.log("counter is: " + counter);
}
```

If you encounter code like this, the most likely situation is that the author forgot to add a line to increment the value of counter. This code will output "counter is: o" until the browser gives up and shows a warning to the user. Here is a better loop that eventually ends:

```javascript
var counter = 0;
while (counter < 10) {
    console.log("counter is: " + counter);
    counter = counter + 1;
}
```

Control Flow

The most common statements after variable declarations are *control flow* statements. These statements instruct the script to follow a particular path, skipping or returning to different blocks of code based on certain criteria.

if/if-else/else

The if keyword lets you make decisions about what your code should do next. You can use any number of conditional expressions to create complex decisions trees.

```
if (expression) {
   console.log("expression is truthy");
} else if (expression2) {
   console.log("expression2 is truthy");
} else if (expression3) {
   console.log("expression3 is truthy");
} else {
   console.log("all of these expressions are falsey");
}
```

switch/case

The switch keyword is another way to make decisions in your code. I
don't use it very often, but here's an example:

```
switch (letter) {
   case "a":
   case "e":
   case "i":
   case "o":
   case "u":
      console.log("letter is definitely a vowel");
      break;
   case "y":
      console.log("letter might be a vowel");
      break;
   default:
      console.log("letter isn't a vowel");
      break;
}
```

This switch statement compares the value of letter to each case, one by one. If the values match, it executes any given code or continues on down the list. The break keyword stops it from continuing any further.

try/catch/finally

Chances are your code will *throw* an error on occasion. Sometimes your code is perfectly valid, but maybe the page is missing an element it relies on. You can trap potential errors and handle them gracefully. The try keyword sets up that trap.

```
try {
    // Declaring a variable without an identifier
    // throws an error
    var;
} catch (exception) {
    // The exception object has a message
    // that describes the error
    console.log(exception);
} finally {
    // This code always runs regardless of
    // whether an error occurred
    console.log("Always executes");
}
```

The finally block of this statement is optional, but the catch block is not.

throw

On occasion, you may want to throw your own errors. This is especially useful when someone else will use your code and you want to alert them when they do something wrong. The throw keyword lets you raise this alert in a way that disrupts the script from continuing (unless you catch the error with a try/catch statement).

```javascript
function argumentRequired(arg) {
    if (arg == null) {
        throw new Error("arg cannot be null or undefined.");
    }
}
argumentRequired(); // Whoops, no argument given
Error: arg cannot be null or undefined.
```

break and continue

Two keywords, break and continue, manage control flow inside loops. The break keywords can stop a loop. This loop runs only while i equals 0, 1, 2, 3, and 4; it stops when it equals 5.

```javascript
for (var i = 0; i < 10; i++) {
    if (i == 5) {
        break;
    }
    console.log(i);
}
```

You can also skip a loop with the continue keyword. This loop runs from 0 to 9 but skips 5:

```javascript
for (var i = 0; i < 10; i++) {
    if (i == 5) {
        continue;
    }
    console.log(i);
}
```

Both of these keywords also work inside while loops.

Compound Expressions

Expressions are the building blocks of JavaScript. Most of the time they're very simple, but like anything else, if you put a whole bunch of them together, they can get pretty complicated.

The simplest expression is a value by itself.

```
16;
16
```

The next-simplest expression contains two values and an operator.

```
15 + 16;
31
```

You can combine any number of values and operators to create complex *compound expressions*. Different data types work with various operators in specific ways. Chapters 2 through 4 will cover important operators for Numbers, Strings, and Arrays, but since all values are "truthy" or "falsey," it's useful to cover the Boolean operators on their own.

Boolean Operators

Boolean operators help manage "truthy" and "falsey" values. They are most useful in `if` statements and the like, but they also have some interesting uses in and of themselves.

Logical NOT: !

The logical NOT operator turns a "truthy" value into `false` and a "falsey" value into `true`. It's another way of determining inequality. These two `if` statements operate identically:

```
if (myVar != true) {
    // It's not true
}
if (! myVar) {
    // It's still not true
}
```

It's useful for determining that something isn't true or that it's missing.

```
var element = document.getElementById("mayNotExist");
if (! element) {
    console.log("The element is falsey, so it must not exist");
}
```

Logical AND: &&

The logical AND operator (&&) takes two operands. It returns the right operand only if the left operand is "truthy." If the left operand is "falsey," it returns that value.

```
var truthyValue = 1;
var falseyValue = null;
// Left operand && right operand
true && truthyValue;
1
falseyValue && truthyValue;
null
```

The interesting thing about the logical AND operator is that it stops evaluating and immediately returns if the left operand is "falsey." Consider this example:

```
function myFunc() {
   alert("executing myFunc!");
   return true;
}
falseyValue && myFunc();
null
```

Because the left operand is "falsey," the expression stops there and doesn't execute myFunc(). In this case, you'll never see the alert dialog box.

This is useful for safeguarding yourself against potential errors. JavaScript will throw an error if you try to access a property on null.

```
var element = document.getElementById("doesNotExist");
element.nodeName;
TypeError: element is null
element && element.nodeName;
null
var element2 = document.getElementById("exists");
element2 && element2.nodeName;
"DIV"
```

Evaluating the nodeName property of a nonexistent element returns an error, but you can quickly determine whether the element exists with the logical AND operator.

Logical OR: ||

The logical OR operator (||) returns the left operand if it's "truthy," and the right operand otherwise. You can think of it as "Keep trying until you find the truth (or something like it)."

```
falseyValue || truthyValue; // Second value
1
truthyValue || falseyValue; // First value
1
false || falseyValue || anotherFalseyValue || truthyValue;
1
```

Combining Boolean Operators

The fun part of Boolean operators comes from combining them to create complex logical expressions.

```
var element = document.body.firstChild;
if (element &&
    (element.nodeName === "DIV" ||
    element.nodeName === "SPAN") &&
    element.childNodes.length) {
    alert("All of these expressions are true");
}
```

Learning to read and write complex expressions like this is a challenge, but it just amounts to understanding the smaller expressions one at a time. Sometimes it helps to store some of the smaller expressions on variables to enhance readability.

```
var isDiv = element && element.nodeName === "DIV"
var isSpan = element && element.nodeName === "SPAN";
var isDivOrSpan = isDiv || isSpan;
if (isDivOrSpan && element.childNodes.length) {
    alert("All of these expressions are true");
}
```

Coding often requires balancing the number of lines and the readability of the code.

Ternary Expressions

Ternary expressions are a slightly more efficient way to manage values based on truthiness. I used them a lot because they let you write a basic if/else statement in one line of code.

```
result = expression ? "it's true" : "it's false";
```

This expression is equivalent to the following:

```
if (expression) {
    result = "it's true";
} else {
    result = "it's false";
}
```

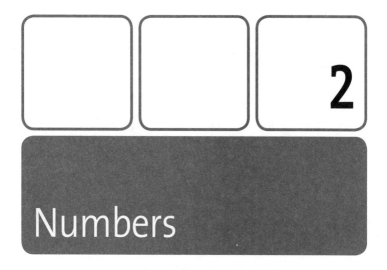

Numbers

There aren't very many surprising aspects to using numbers and math in JavaScript. In fact, most of my scripts use numbers for little more than counters and simple addition. But when you're creating complex layouts or programming animation, it's helpful to know the ins and outs of numbers in JavaScript.

Basic Math

Most of the time you use numbers for simple math, using familiar operators.

```
1 + 2; // Addition
3
5.1 * -10.5; // Multiplication
-53.55
100 - 10; // Subtraction
90
2 / 3; // Division
0.6666666666666666
10 % 4; // Modulus, or the remainder of 10 / 4
2
```

The modulus operator (%) is great for determining whether a number is odd or even.

```
if (num % 2 === 1) {
    console.log("num is odd");
} else {
    console.log("num is even");
}
```

Operators have a specific precedence, just like we all learned in algebra class. You can use parentheses to ensure you get the desired result.

```
1 + 2 * 3;
7
(1 + 2) * 3;
9
```

The increment (++) and decrement (--) operators work differently on the left side of a variable than on the right.

```
var first = 0;
var second = first++;
[first, second];
[1, 0]
```

In the previous example, the value of first is assigned to second *before* the increment operator adds 1. Put the operator on the other side of the variable, and you'll get a different result, as shown here:

```
var first = 0;
var second = ++second;
[first, second];
[1, 1]
```

This time, the value of first is assigned to second *after* incrementing by 1.

Most math operators have *assignment* versions, which perform the operation and assign the value to the same variable with one operator.

```
var num = 2;
num += 5; // Same as num = num + 5;
7
num /= 2;
3.5
num *= 4;
14
num -= 5;
9
num %= 2;
1
```

Number Formats

You can express numbers in a few different ways, though I rarely have a reason to do so. JavaScript doesn't differentiate between integers and real numbers. I tend to refer to numbers with decimal points as *floating-point* numbers, though technically all numbers are floating-point numbers.

```
var myInteger = 16;
var myFloat = 1.08;
```

If you need to express really big or really small numbers, you can use scientific notation.

```
var reallyBig = 8.67e100;
var reallySmall = 15e-42;
```

Most JavaScript numbers use the base-10 number system, but you can also express numbers in base-8 or base-16. Base-8 numbers start with a zero and only use zero through seven. Base-16 numbers start with 0x or 0X and use zero through nine and A through F. Colors are often expressed in base-16, or *hexadecimal*, digits.

```
0123; // Base-8
83
0xFFF; // Base-16
4095
```

Be careful not to start numbers with a zero unless you really mean to express a base-8 number!

Constants and Functions

JavaScript has a number of built-in constants and functions that you can use:

- **isNaN(x)** Returns true if x is not a number or easily converted to a number.

- **Number.MAX_VALUE** The largest number you can express in JavaScript.

- **Number.MIN_VALUE** The lowest negative number you can express in JavaScript.

- **Infinity** A global variable that represents infinity. This is the result if you try to divide by zero.

The Math Object

The Math object provides many constants and functions for more complex operations.

- **Math.PI** An approximate value of pi

- **Math.abs(x)** The absolute value of x

- **Math.ceil(x)** The closest integer greater than x

- **Math.floor(x)** The closest integer less than x

- **Math.max(x, y, ...)** The largest of all arguments

- **Math.min(x, y, ...)** The smallest of all arguments

- **Math.random()** A pseudorandom number between 0 and 1

- **Math.round(x)** The closest integer to x

- **Math.sqrt(x)** The square root of x

Even More Properties and Methods

The following lesser-used Math properties and methods are good for more complex math and trigonometry:

Math.E	Math.SQRT2	Math.exp()
Math.LN10	Math.acos()	Math.log()
Math.LN2	Math.asin()	Math.pow()
Math.LOG10E	Math.atan()	Math.sin()
Math.LOG2E	Math.atan2()	Math.tan()
Math.SQRT1_2	Math.cos()	

Generating Random Integers

Math.random() only returns numbers between zero and one, but you can easily generate a random integer between two integers with a little extra math.

```
var lower = 2;
var higher = 10;
Math.round(Math.random() * (higher - lower)) + lower;
```

Conversion

Because JavaScript is a "loosely typed" language, data changes from one type to another easily. This lets you use Booleans, Numbers, and Strings interchangeably in many cases. Some values don't easily convert to another data type, however, so it's useful to understand the conversion rules.

The easiest way to convert a number to a string is add a string to it.

```
var myNumber = 42;
typeof myNumber;
"number"
myNumber + "";
"42"
typeof (myNumber + "");
"string"
```

Any time you use a number in a string context, it's automatically converted to a string. But be careful because this is another place where operator precedent rules come into play.

```
"The answer is " + 40 + 2;
"The answer is 402"
"The answer is " + (40 + 2);
"The answer is 42"
```

Converting strings to numbers can be a little trickier. If the string is basically a number primitive wrapped in quotes, you can put the *unary plus* (+) operator in front of it.

```
+"1.5";
1.5
+"5px";
NaN
```

If the string contains any non-numeric characters, the result is NaN, or Not a Number. You can test for this with the isNaN() function.

```
isNaN("5px");
true
isNaN("123456");
false
```

The parseInt() and parseFloat() functions are more flexible but may also return NaN.

```
parseInt("5.1 inches", 10);
5
parseFloat("1.5f", 10);
1.5
parseInt("a1", 10);
NaN
```

The second argument is the *radix*, or the base system you're using. It's almost always 10, unless you are parsing a base-8 or base-16 number. If your number starts with a zero, make sure to define the radix.

```
parseInt("07");
0
parseInt("07", 10);
7
```

You can use the toFixed() method to convert a number to a string and determine the number of decimal places displayed.

```
var interest = 100 * 2.95 / 12;
interest.toFixed(0);
"24"
interest.toFixed(2);
"24.58"
```

Number Precision

JavaScript is a great language for many things, but I don't recommend using it to design your trip to the moon. You might crash and burn if your calculations work out like this:

```
0.1 + 0.2;
0.30000000000000004
```

The floating-point number system in JavaScript is flawed and introduces tiny rounding errors in many operations. To be honest, you probably will not need that much accuracy in your code, but it's still worth noting.

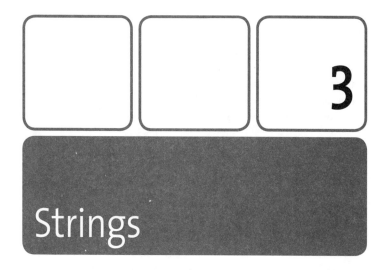

3

Strings

The Web is made up of text: HTTP is a text-based protocol, and browsers consume Web content in HTML text files. JavaScript handles text in a flexible, capable manner with the powerful String data type.

Escape Characters

You can surround characters with either single primes (') or double primes (") to create a string. But whichever symbol you use, you can't use it again in the middle of the string because that will end the string early. However, you can *escape* any character with a backslash (\) to solve this or use single primes inside double primes (and vice versa).

```
"He said "hello!"";
SyntaxError: missing ; before statement
"She said \"hello!\"";
"She said "hello!""
'They say "hello!"';
"They say "hello!""
```

Escape sequences are useful for other things too, such as for newlines (\n), tabs (\t), and Unicode character codes (\u00A3 is £ and \u2603 is ☃).

Operators

The plus sign (+) operator concatenates strings together. Concatenation isn't the same as addition, so watch out when you're adding strings and numbers together.

```
"hello" + " world";
"hello world"
"2" + "2";
"22"
```

Like numbers, the plus operator also has an assignment version (+=) so you can concatenate a string in place. These two examples are identical if myString equals "hello".

```
myString = myString + " world";
"hello world"
myString += " world";
"hello world"
```

The greater-than (>) and less-than (<) operators compare strings in alphabetical order...sort of. A is less than Z, but uppercase letters are "lower" than lowercase letters, so Z is less than a.

```
"Alpha" < "Zeta";
true
"Zeta" > "alpha";
false
```

Properties

Strings have one built-in property, length, which is the number of characters in a string.

```
"abcdefghijklmnopqrstuvwxyz".length;
26
```

Methods

All string methods return a new string, leaving the original string unchanged.

```
var myString = "hello";
var myTransformedString = myString.toUpperCase();
myTransformedString;
"HELLO"
myString; // Remains the same
"hello"
```

Changing Case: toUpperCase(), toLowerCase()

The methods toUpperCase() and toLowerCase() are pretty self-evident. I mentioned earlier that uppercase letters are "lower" than lowercase letters, so these methods are useful when you want to reliably compare strings in alphabetical order.

```
var string1 = "B comes after (is greater than) a";
var string2 = "a comes before (is less than) b";

string1 > string2;
false
string1.toLowerCase() > string2.toLowerCase();
true
string2.toUpperCase() < string1.toUpperCase();
true
```

It doesn't really matter which method you use as long as you're consistent.

Extracting Parts of a String

Extracting bits and pieces from strings is such a common task that JavaScript has several functions for doing so. Some of these functions are so similar that you'll want to return to the following sections when you need a reminder of the distinctions between them.

charAt(x), charCodeAt(x)

The charAt() method returns a string with the character at the specified index in the string. Like arrays, indices start at zero.

```
"abcde".charAt(0);
"a"
```

```
"abcde".charAt(3);
"d"
// Using an index greater than the string's length
"abcde".charAt(10);
""
```

The charCodeAt() method is similar, except that it returns the numeric encoding for the found character. You'll see in Chapter 11 that key presses are returned as character encodings, so it's helpful to know how to convert characters and character codes.

```
"a".charCodeAt(0);
97
```

The fromCharCode() method is available on the String object—not on a specific string instance—to turn a character code back into string.

```
String.fromCharCode(97);
"a"
```

slice(x[, y])

note   When I specify function arguments in brackets, as in (x[, y]), I'm indicating that those arguments are optional. In this case, y is optional but x is not. The brackets aren't part of the code, but the parentheses are.

The slice() method returns a subsection of the string, starting at position x and including the characters up to (but not including) position y. The arguments can both be negative, which means that they start counting the position from the end of the string instead of the beginning. If the second argument isn't specified, slice(x) returns the subsection of the string starting at position x through the end of the string.

```
"abcde".slice(0, 2);
"ab"
"abcde".slice(1, -1);
"bcd"
"abcde".slice(-2);
"de"
```

substr(x[, y])

The substr() method is similar to slice() except that y is the *length*
of the resulting substring instead of the position at which the substring
ends. The first argument can still be negative, and the second argument
is still optional.

```
// Looks the same as slice
"abcde".substr(0, 2);
"ab"
// Not the same; specifies the length of the substring
"abcde".substr(1, 3);
"bcd"
// Since the second argument is still
// optional, it looks the same as slice
"abcde".substr(-2);
"de"
```

Converting Strings to Arrays: split([*delimiter, limit*])

The split() method breaks a string up into parts and returns an array.
The delimiter argument determines where to split the string. If the
delimiter isn't specified, it returns an array containing the whole string as
its first item.

```
"a,b,c,d,e".split(","); // Split on commas
```

```
["a", "b", "c", "d", "e"]
"a sentence split by words".split(" "); // Split on spaces
["a", "sentence", "split", "by", "words"]
"|a|b|c|".split("|"); // The parts can be empty strings
["", "a", "b", "c", ""]
"a,b,c,d,e".split(); // No delimiter
["a,b,c,d,e"]
```

If you specify a numeric limit as the second argument, the resulting array contains only the specified number of items.

```
"a,b,c,d,e".split(",", 3);
["a", "b", "c"]
```

Search and Replace

You often need to know whether a string contains another string or matches a certain pattern. Once you've found the string or pattern, you can replace it with another string. It's surprising how many different ways you can use the following methods.

indexOf(substring[, start])

The indexOf() method returns the position of the first occurrence of a substring. If the substring doesn't exist inside the string, it returns -1. If you specify a start argument, it starts searching for the substring after that position in the string.

```
"hello world".indexOf("world");
6
"hello world".indexOf("World"); // It's case sensitive
-1
"hello world".indexOf("o", 5); // Skips the first o
7
```

The fact that indexOf() returns -1 instead of false can easily trip you up. If you're not careful, you can write code that works exactly the opposite of how you would expect.

```javascript
var myString = "hello world";
// If the string does *not* contain the substring:
if (! myString.indexOf("not found")) {
    console.log("Substring not found!");
}

// If the string *does* contain the substring:
if (myString.indexOf("hello")) {
    console.log("String contains 'hello'");
}
```

In the first example of the previous code, indexOf() doesn't find the substring and returns -1, which is a "truthy" value. I wanted to print to the console if I couldn't find the substring, but because I used the not (!) operator, it does the opposite of what I expect.

In the second example of the previous code, indexOf() finds the substring at position 0, which is a "falsey" value. Because the substring is the start of myString, this test also does the opposite of what I expect.

The only safe way to use indexOf() is to test explicitly against -1, as shown here:

```javascript
if (myString.indexOf("not found") === -1) {
    console.log("Substring not found!");
}

if (myString.indexOf("hello") !== -1) {
    console.log("String contains 'hello'");
}
```

lastIndexOf(substring[, start])

The `lastIndexOf()` method is the same as `indexOf()` except that it starts searching at the end of the string instead of at the beginning.

```
"hello world".lastIndexOf("o");
7
```

Regular Expressions

The following methods, `search()`, `match()`, and `replace()`, get their power from another built-in JavaScript data type: Regular Expressions.

Regular expressions, or *RegExps*, are complicated enough to basically be a mini-language inside JavaScript. It takes a while to get the hang of them—far longer than I can cover in this book. I'll explain the regular expressions used in my examples, but I recommend looking for examples, tutorials, and reference material in other books and online.

JavaScript regular expressions have a lot of features, but they aren't as fully featured as Perl-compatible regular expressions and RegExp engines found in other languages. Make sure you're looking for references and examples specifically for the JavaScript language.

A regular expression describes a pattern. You can search for that pattern in a string. The most basic pattern is a series of alphanumeric characters.

```
var myPattern = /matching characters/;
```

Regular expressions sort of look like strings, except they use forward slashes (/) instead of quote marks to delineate the beginning and end. Like strings, you have to escape special characters with backslashes (\). Unlike strings, there are several special characters in regular expressions: ^ $. * + ? = ! : | \ / ( ) [ ] { }.

search(regexp)

The search() method is the same as indexOf() except that it takes a regular expression pattern instead of a substring. It also returns -1 if the pattern isn't found.

```
"hello world".search(/[aeiou]/); // Find the first vowel
1
"hello world".search(/\d/); // Find the first digit
-1
```

match(regexp)

The match() method returns an array containing all the substrings matching the regular expression and its subpatterns. Unlike the other search-and-replace methods, it returns null if the pattern doesn't match. Here are some simple examples, but I'll cover this function more in Chapter 8:

```
// Find all the vowels
"hello world".match(/[aeiou]/g);
["e", "o", "o"]
// Find "world" regardless of capitalization
"hElLo WoRlD".match(/world/i);
["WoRlD"]
```

replace(pattern, replacement)

The replace() method works like match() except that it returns a string with all instances of pattern replaced by the string replacement.

```
// Remove all non-numeric characters from a phone number
"(310) 555-9876".replace(/\D/g, "");
"3105559876"
```

The pattern argument can just be a simple substring instead of a regular expression, but it will replace only the first occurrence.

```
"favorite color: red".replace("red", "blue");
"favorite color: blue"
```

To replace every occurrence, use a pattern with the global (g) option.

```
// Without using the global option
"red, red, red".replace(/red/, "blue");
"blue, red, red"
"red, red, red".replace(/red/g, "blue");
"blue, blue, blue"
```

If the pattern argument has subpatterns, you can access them in the replacement string with placeholders in the form of $1 up to $99.

```
// \w+ matches multiple "word" characters,
// like letters and numbers. That word is inserted
// into the replacement with the $1 placeholder
"Name: Lenny".replace(/Name: (\w+)/, "Hi $1!");
"Hi Lenny!"
```

The replacement argument can also be a function that returns a string. The following sample matches all lowercase vowels and replaces them with uppercased vowels:

```
var replacementFunc = function(vowel) {
    return vowel.toUpperCase();
};
"hello world".replace(/[aeiou]/g, replacementFunc);
"hEllO wOrld"
```

Helper Functions

The JavaScript language is relatively small. Sometimes you need to add your own functions to expand the operations you can perform. Here is just one example.

stringTrim()

JavaScript didn't include a method for trimming whitespace off the beginning and ending of a string until recently, so for most browsers you have to provide your own. The jQuery library includes this helper function (where it is available as jQuery.trim()).

```
function stringTrim(s) {
    return s.replace(/^(\s|\u00A0)+|(\s|\u00A0)+$/g, "");
}

stringTrim(" hello ");
"hello"
```

You'll learn how to turn this into a string method in the "Prototype" section of Chapter 6.

Global Functions

JavaScript includes a few global functions for encoding and decoding strings.

escape(string), unescape(string)

The escape() function converts most special characters to hexadecimal character codes. It leaves letters, digits, and the following characters alone:

@ * _ + - . /

Hexadecimal character codes look like %20 (which represents a space) or %u20AC (which represents €).

The unescape() function performs the reverse operation.

encodeURI(string), decodeURI(string)

The encodeURI() method is similar to escape(), but it's specifically meant for encoding Web addresses. It converts all characters to hexadecimal characters codes except letters, digits, and the following characters:

@ * _ + - . / ! ~ ` ( ) ; / ? : & = , #

This function assumes you're encoding a full URL.

The decodeURI() function performs the reverse operation.

encodeURIComponent(string), decodeURIComponent(string)

The encodeURIComponent() function is the most useful of these global string functions. It converts all characters to hexadecimal character codes except letters, digits, and the following characters:

- _ . ! ~ * ` ( )

This function encodes characters that separate different components of a URL, so you can safely encode a string for use as a single component. This is most commonly used for encoding a string for use as a query string value. You can even encode a URL as a query string parameter.

```
var value = "http://www.other.com/?param=1&param2=2";
var encodedValue = encodeURIComponent(value);
"http://www.example.com/redirect?url=" + encodedValue;
"http://www.example.com/redirect?url=
➥http%3A%2F%2Fwww.example.com%2F%3Fparam%3D1%26param%3D2"
```

Without encoding value, the "&param2=2" part of the string would be interpreted as a second query string parameter instead of part of the ?url= value.

4

Arrays

Arrays are a great tool for organizing and manipulating a lot of data. JavaScript arrays can store any of the JavaScript data types in any order. If you store your data in arrays, operating on it is simply a matter of looping over each value. It's a simple operation, but you'll find that arrays and loops have endless uses in JavaScript programming.

Creating Arrays

The best way to create a new array is with the array literal syntax ([]), but the array constructor function is available too. If you pass a single number value to the constructor function, you get an array filled with that many undefined values.

```
var myArray = [];
var myFilledArray = new Array(4);
myFilledArray;
[undefined, undefined, undefined, undefined]
```

Properties

Like strings, arrays have one built-in property: length. This property is equal to the number greater than the last index in the array. This is true even if you skip some indices.

```
["a", 1, true, null].length;
4
var myArray = [];
myArray.length;
0
myArray[99] = 1;
1
myArray.length;
100
```

The new length of myArray is 100 even though it contains only one value at index 99. All the other values are undefined.

The following is the quickest way to add an item to the end of an array, since the length property is one greater than the index of the last item:

```
myArray = ["a","b","c"];
// Same as myArray[3] = "d"
myArray[myArray.length] = "d";
```

Looping Over Arrays

Looping over arrays is one of the most common tasks in JavaScript, and
there are dozens of ways to do it. In my code, I stick to just two versions
for readability and performance reasons.

Both versions use the for statement. The simpler of the two should look
familiar from Chapter 1, as shown here:

```
var myArray = [1, 2, 3, 4, 5];
for (var i = 0, l = myArray.length; i < l; i++) {
    console.log(myArray[i]);
}
```

The one important difference is in the *setup* expression, where I declare
both i and l at the same time. I do this because the *test* is executed
every time the loop runs, and I can save a few milliseconds by saving the
value of length to a variable from the start.

My second favorite loop pattern can be used only if every element in the
array is "truthy" (not zero, false, an empty string, null, or undefined), so I
use it only in special cases. The most common case is when I'm looping
over elements in a page.

```
// Get a collection of <a> tags from the page
// and loop over them
var allLinks = document.getElementsByTagName("a");
for (var i = -1, link; link = allLinks[++i];) {
    console.log(link);
}
```

Make sure you run this in a page that actually has links, or you won't see any output!

The previous is still a normal for loop, but I'm doing some tricky things in each expression:

- In the *setup*, I declare i as −1 and link as undefined (it doesn't need a value yet).

- In the *test*, I access the next link in the allLinks collection by incrementing i and using the bracket operators ([]). The first time this happens, -1 becomes 0 and returns the first item in allLinks. I then assign that value to link.

  Note that I use the increment (++) operator on the left side of i so that I add 1 to i *before* evaluating it in the brackets.

- In the *increment* expression, I don't do anything because I already incremented i in the *test*. Note that the semicolon is still required after the test.

I like this usage of the for loop because I don't need to worry about i in the body of the loop. I have the link variable to work with as soon as possible. It's also a great demonstration of the flexibility of JavaScript.

forEach(loopFunc)

Looping over arrays using functions is increasingly common, especially in certain libraries. Modern browsers support the forEach() method, but you can also build your own.

```
function arrayForEach(array, loopFunc) {
    // If the browser support forEach, use it because
    // it will be faster
    if ("forEach" in array) {
        return array.forEach(loopFunc);
```

```
    // Otherwise, loop over the array and pass in
    // the array values to the loop function
    } else {
        for (var i = 0, l = array.length; i < l; i++) {
            loopFunc(array[i], i, array);
        }
        return array;
    }
}

function doSomeMath(num) {
    console.log(num * 10 - 5);
}

arrayForEach([1,2,3], doSomeMath);
5
15
25
```

Methods

Unlike string methods, some array methods change the original array while returning a separate value.

Adding Items to Arrays

Earlier, I showed you how to quickly add a value to the end of an array using the length property. JavaScript also provides a few different methods for adding values to both ends of an array.

concat(x[, y , z ...])

The concat() method concatenates values to the end of the array and returns the result. The original array doesn't change. You can pass in any number of arguments. If an argument is an array, each value is concatenated individually.

```
[1, 2, 3].concat(4, [5, 6]);
[1, 2, 3, 4, 5, 6]
```

push(x[, y, z ...])

The push() method is the same as the concat() method except for a few differences:

- It *does* change the original array.
- It returns the new length of the array.
- If an argument is an array, it does *not* concatenate each value individually.

```
var myArray = ["a", "b", "c"];
myArray.push("d", ["e", "f"]);
5
myArray;
["a", "b", "c", "d", ["e", "f"]]
```

unshift(x[, y, z ...])

The unshift() method is exactly the same as push() except that it adds values to the beginning of the array instead of the end.

```
var myArray = ["d", "e", "f"];
myArray.unshift("a", ["b", "c"]);
5
```

```
myArray;
["a", ["b", "c"], "d", "e", "f"]
```

Removing Items from Arrays

The push() and unshift() methods have analogs for removing values from the ends of an array.

pop()

The pop() method is the opposite of push(). It returns one element removed from the end of the array. It *does* change the original array, including its length property.

```
var myArray = ["a", "b", "c"];
myArray.pop();
"c"
myArray;
["a", "b"]
```

shift()

Unsurprisingly, the shift() method is the opposite of unshift().

```
var myArray = ["a", "b", "c"];
myArray.shift();
"a"
myArray;
["b", "c"]
```

Extracting Items from Arrays

The slice() and splice() methods are very useful for manipulating arrays. It's easy to forget which method is which, even though they work in very different ways.

slice(x[, y])

The slice() method works the same for arrays as it does for strings. It
returns a new array starting with the value at the index x up to but not
including the value at the index y. It doesn't change the original array.
The arguments can both be negative, which counts the position from
the end of the array. The second argument is optional, returning an array
from x until the end of the array.

```
["a", "b", "c", "d", "e"].slice(0, 2);
["a", "b"]
["a", "b", "c", "d", "e"].slice(1, -1);
["b", "c", "d"]
["a", "b", "c", "d", "e"].slice(-2);
["d", "e"]
```

splice(start[, length, newValue ...])

The splice() method deletes a specified number of values from an array
and optionally inserts new values in their place. It changes the original
array and returns a new array containing any deleted values.

If you provide only the start argument, splice() deletes all the values
from start until the end of the array. The start argument can be negative, counting the starting index from the end of the array.

```
var myArray = ["a", "b", "c", "d", "e"];
myArray.splice(2); // Start deleting at "c"
["c", "d", "e"]
myArray;
["a", "b"]
```

If you also provide the length argument, splice() deletes only that number of values.

```
var myArray = ["a", "b", "c", "d", "e"];
myArray.splice(2, 2); // Delete 2 values starting at "c"
["c", "d"]
myArray;
["a", "b", "e"]
```

If you provide any more arguments, those values are inserted in the array in the place of the deleted values.

```
var myArray = ["a", "b", "c", "d", "e"];
// Insert these values after
// deleting 2 values starting at "c"
myArray.splice(2, 2, "x", "y", "z");
["c", "d"]
myArray;
["a", "b", "x", "y", "z", "e"]
```

You can specify the length argument as zero to insert elements at an arbitrary point in the array.

```
var myArray = ["a", "b", "c"];
myArray.splice(2, 0, "x", "y"); // Delete 0 values
[]
myArray;
["a", "b", "x", "y", "c"]
```

Ordering Arrays

Sometimes you may want to present the values of an array to the user in a particular order. These methods come in handy for simple and complex array sorting.

reverse()

The reverse() method reverses the order of the values in the array. It changes the original array and returns a reference to the same array.

```
var myArray = [1, 2, 3];
myArray.reverse();
[3, 2, 1]
```

sort([func]*)*

By default, the sort() method reorders the values in the array alphabetically, with lowercase letters being higher than uppercase. With numbers, this is not the expected behavior:

```
[222, 3, 11].sort();
[11, 222, 3]
```

Fortunately, you can pass a function as an argument that sorts the array however you like.

```
function numericalSort(a, b) {
    return a - b;
}
[222, 3, 11].sort(numericalSort);
[3, 11, 222]
```

The sorting function must return the following:

- A number greater than zero if a is greater than b

- A number less than zero if a is less than b

- Zero if a equals b

You can also sort arbitrary objects this way.

```
var gum = { price : 0.79 };
var mints = { price : 1.29 };
var candy = { price : 1.49 };
var products = [mints, candy, gum];
products.sort(function(a, b) {
    return a.price - b.price;
});
[Object price=0.79, Object price=1.29, Object price=1.49]
```

note In this example, I passed an anonymous function to the sort() method instead of a reference to a declared function. If you need to use a function only once, this is a great style to adopt.

The sort() function changes the original array and returns a reference to the same array.

Converting Arrays to Strings

Strings have the split() function, so it makes sense that arrays would have a method to perform the opposite operation.

join([delimiter]*)*

The join() method is the opposite of the split() method for strings. It turns each value of an array into strings and concatenates them together with commas between each value. The optional delimiter argument can change the comma to any other string.

```
["a", "b", "c"].join();
"a,b,c"
["a", "b", "c"].join("--");
"a--b--c"
["a", ["b", "c"]].join("+");
"a+b,c"
```

In the third example of the previous code, the second value of the array is another array. Before joining the values with "+", it converts the ["b", "c"] array into a string with the toString() method, which may not be the expected result.

Joining string values together is a great way to create long strings out of many parts. Consider these two examples:

```
var longString = "";
for (var i = 0; i < 100; i++) {
    longString += "shorter string no. " + i + "\n";
}

var stringArray = [];
for (var i = 0; i < 100; i++) {
    stringArray.push("shorter string no. " + i);
}
var longString = stringArray.join("\n");
```

The second example is often slightly faster, especially in Internet Explorer.

toString()

The toString() method acts just like join() with no arguments.

Functions

Functions are remarkably flexible in JavaScript. That flexibility provides a lot of power, but it can also create confusion, especially in how functions interact with variables and objects. This chapter covers some pretty advanced concepts; some nuances might not stick with you right away, but once you spend some time with functions, you'll really start to appreciate the power of the JavaScript language.

Creating Functions

The two ways to create functions both use the function keyword, so the differences between them aren't immediately apparent.

Declarations

Variable declarations and function declarations operate similarly. They start with a keyword (var or function), followed by an identifier. Function declarations add lists of arguments in parentheses followed by blocks in curly braces.

```
function functionName(arg1, arg2, argN) {
    // Block of statements
}
```

JavaScript interpreters look at function declarations before everything else in the script, so you can call them even before you declare them.

```
myFunc();

function myFunc() {
    // Statements
}
```

Expressions

You don't have to declare a name for a function, though the following example is pretty useless (and requires extra parentheses so as not to throw an error):

```
(function() {
    // Statements
});
```

Functions expressed without a name are *function expressions* and are
sometimes referred to as *anonymous functions*. You can store a function
expression on a variable or use it as a return value in another function.

```
var functionName = function(arg1, arg2, argN) {
    // Statements
};

function outerFunction() {
    // This function returns an anonymous function
    return function() {
        console.log("inner function");
    };
}
```

> **note** You don't need to put a semicolon after the closing curly bracket in a
> function declaration. Function expressions, on the other hand, should
> always end with a semicolon.

Self-invoking Functions

Sometimes you may want to call a function immediately, for reasons
explained in the "Closures" section later in this chapter.

```
(function() {
    // Executed immediately
})();
```

You can't immediately invoke a function declaration, so parentheses
are required around the function to indicate that this is a function
expression.

Arguments

Function arguments are very flexible in JavaScript. Named arguments in the function signature are just for convenience more than anything else. You don't need to provide a value for each argument.

```
function myFunc(arg0, arg1, arg2) {
    console.log(arg0);
    console.log(arg1);
    console.log(arg2);
}

myFunc("a", "b"); // Left off the third argument
"a"
"b"
undefined
```

You can also provide more argument values than defined in the function signature. All of the arguments are stored in a local variable called arguments for easy access.

```
function myFunc(arg0) {
    console.log(arg0);
    console.log(arguments[1]); // The second argument
    console.log(arguments[2]); // The third argument
}

myFunc("a", "b", "c");
"a"
"b"
"c"
```

The `arguments` variable is an arraylike object but isn't a true array. If you ever want to use an array method like `pop()`, you'll need to convert it to an array by looping over each item and adding it to a real array.

> **note** Arraylike objects are often referred to as *collections*. You access their properties by numeric indices (`arguments[0]` and so forth), and they have a `length` property, but they don't have any of the array methods discussed in Chapter 3.

Default Values for Arguments

Since arguments are optional, you may want to provide default values. In most cases, you can use the logical OR (||) operator to assign a value if it doesn't already exist.

```
function sayHello(name) {
    name = name || "Lenny";
    console.log("Hi " + name + "!");
}

sayHello();
"Hi Lenny!"
sayHello("Sally");
"Hi Sally!";
```

In the first line of the function, if `name` is "falsey," it assigns "Lenny" to the variable. When you call `sayHello()` without specifying a value for `name`, its value is undefined, which is "falsey."

But what if it's perfectly valid for an argument to be "falsey"? The following function doesn't work as expected:

```
function trueUnlessSpecifed(answer) {
   // If answer isn't provided, it defaults to true
   answer = answer || true;
   console.log(answer);
}

trueUnlessSpecifed(false);
true
```

The variable = variable || defaultValue pattern doesn't work here because a "falsey" value is always changed to the default. The safest way to assign a default value is to check whether the argument is truly undefined. In the following function, an unspecified answer argument will default to true:

```
function trueUnlessSpecifed(answer) {
   answer = answer == undefined ? true : answer;
   console.log(answer);
}

trueUnlessSpecifed();
true
trueUnlessSpecifed(false);
false
```

note Remember that this pattern: expression ? ifTrue : ifFalse;

is similar to the following: if (expression) {
                                  ifTrue;
                              } else {
                                 ifFalse;
                              }

Objects as Arguments

You may want to write functions that take many arguments, some of which are optional.

```
function drawElement(color, border, width, height,
                     left, top, zIndex) {
   // Make and display an element with these variables
}
drawElement("red", 4, null, null, 100, 10);
```

Function signatures like this aren't ideal for a couple of reasons:

- It's hard to remember the exact order of arguments.

- You have to specify null values when you want to use the default value for arguments in the middle of the signature.

- Did you notice that I forgot to specify a value for zIndex? It's hard to count all those arguments correctly!

Passing multiple values in a single object is often a better solution:

```
function drawElement(options) {
   // Make and display an element with the values in options
}
drawElement({
   color: "red",
   border: 4,
   left: 100,
   top: 10
});
```

Specifying default values is a little bit trickier with this technique. You'll need to create an object holding all the defaults and merge it with the options object.

```
drawElement.DEFAULTS = {
    color: "blue",
    border: 0
    width: 50,
    height: 50,
    left: 0,
    top: 0,
    zIndex: 1
};
```

You can store the defaults as property of the function itself. Using all capital letters is a hint to other coders that these values shouldn't be changed.

```
function mergeOptions(defaults, options) {
    // Use the for/in statement to loop over the property
    // names in defaults
    for (var name in defaults) {

        // See Chapter 6 for the reason behind
        // this "if" statement
        if (defaults.hasOwnProperty(name)) {

            // If the property doesn't exist on options,
            // add it using the value on defaults
            if (options[name] == null) {
                options[name] = defaults[name];
            }
        }
    }
    return options;
}
```

```
function drawElement(options) {
    options = mergeOptions(drawElement.DEFAULTS, options);
    // Make and display an element with the values in options
}
```

Return Values

All functions return a value, but that value is undefined unless you specify it with the return keyword.

```
function noReturn() {
    // Don't explicitly use return
}

// Tests the return value, not the function
typeof noReturn();
"undefined"

function withReturn() {
    return 42;
}

withReturn();
42
```

You can use the return keyword at any point in a function, even to exit the function early. Consider these two functions:

```
function oddOrEven(num) {
    if (num % 2 === 1) {
        var result = "odd";
    } else {
```
(continues on next page)

```
        var result = "even";
    }
    return result;
}

function oddOrEven(num) {
    if (num % 2 === 1) {
        return "odd";
    }
    return "even";
}
```

Returning the result immediately makes your functions shorter and
easier to understand.

Functions as Methods

Functions always have a context when they're called, which is accessible via the this keyword. This is one of the more confusing concepts in
JavaScript, so I'll start with some illustrative examples.

```
function globalFunc() {
    console.log(this);
}

globalFunc();
Window
```

When you call a function normally, its context is the global object. (See
Chapter 8 on the window object for a discussion of the global object.)

```
var myObject = {
    someProperty: 42
};
myObject.method = function() {
    console.log(this.someProperty);
};

myObject.method();
42
```

When a function is a property of an object, it's referred to as a *method*. Calling that function with the dot (.) operator on the object changes the function's context. In this case, this refers to myObject.

This is how built-in methods change the object they're called on. You could create your own push() method for an array like this:

```
var myArray = [];
myArray.myPush = function(obj) {
    this[this.length] = obj;
    return this.length;
}

myArray.myPush(1);
myArray.myPush(2);
myArray.push(3);
myArray;
[1, 2, 3]
```

note Of course, this implementation of push() is incomplete, since you should be able to pass in any number of arguments. Try adding this functionality. (Hint: Loop over the arguments variable.)

Functions can lose their context very easily.

```
var myObject = {
    someProperty: 42
};
myObject.method = function() {
    console.log(this.someProperty);
};

var objectMethod = myObject.method;
objectMethod();
undefined
```

Here, the example stored a reference to the object's method on a variable and then called it without using the dot operator. This causes the function's context to change back to the global object. Since window doesn't have a property called someProperty, it returns undefined.

These concepts are extremely important because JavaScript code is event-based and asynchronous, which means that you're passing functions around and waiting for them to be executed in an eventual context. See Chapter 13 to learn more about this.

Context Binding

JavaScript is one of a small number of languages that gives you the ability to manage function context. Functions have two methods of their own, call() and apply(), which allow you to execute them in a certain context.

```
function calledFunc() {
    console.log(this.someProperty);
}
```

```
var myObject = {
    someProperty : 42
};

calledFunc.call(myObject);
42
calledFunc.apply(myObject);
42
```

The first argument for both call() and apply() is the context object for the function.

You can also pass in arguments to the function with these methods, as shown here:

```
function adder(num1, num2) {
    return this.value + num1 + num2;
}

adder.call(myObject, 10, 20);
72
```

The values 10 and 20 are passed in as the arguments num1 and num2. The apply() method handles this a little differently:

```
adder.apply(myObject, [10, 20]);
72
```

The apply() method lets us pass in all the arguments as a single array. Here's an example that uses Math.max() to find the largest number in an array in one function call:

```
var numbers = [4, 8, 15, 16, 23, 42];
Math.max.apply(Math, numbers);
42
```

Closures

Functions in JavaScript have *lexical scope*, which means that they maintain access to the scope they are declared in. This is also a confusing topic, so here's an example:

```
function scopeFunc() {
   var scopedVar = 42;

   function innerFunc() {
      console.log(scopedVar);
   };

   return innerFunc;
};

var closure = scopeFunc();
closure();
42
```

It breaks down like this:

1. You declare the variable scopedVar inside scopeFunc(). This means you cannot access scopedVar outside scopeFunc().

2. You also declare the function innerFunc() inside scopeFunc(). Since it is in the same scope as scopedVar, it still has access to that variable.

3. You return a reference to innerFunc() when scopeFunc() executes.

4. You save the returned reference to innerFunc() on the variable closure. When you execute the function, it still has access to scopedVar and prints its value to the console.

These inner functions are called *closures* because they "close over" the variables in their scope. This is a very powerful organizational tool, especially when you want to keep different pieces of code separate. It allows you to create "private" variables and functions and control access to them by selectively returning certain references.

One simple practical example is creating a function that returns a unique string every time it runs, like this:

```
var uniqueId = (function() {
    var counter = 0;

    return function() {
        return "unique-id-" + counter++;
    };
})(); // Self-invoking function executes automatically

uniqueId();
"unique-id-0"
uniqueId();
"unique-id-1"
uniqueId();
"unique-id-2"
```

The uniqueId variable holds a reference to the anonymous function, which is the only object that has access to the counter variable. You can be sure that nothing else can change counter and every string returned is unique.

Another practical example is a little more complicated and therefore usually trips up novice JavaScript coders. This code uses objects and functions you'll find in Chapters 10 and 11 later in the book.

```
for (var i = 0; i < 10; i++) {
    var link = document.createElement("a");
    link.innerHTML = "Link " + i;
    link.href = "#";
    link.onclick = function() {
        alert("This is link " + i);
        return false;
    };
    document.body.appendChild(link);
}
```

This for loop creates 10 <a> elements and appends them to the body of the page. (If you're typing this into the Firebug console, you may have to scroll to the bottom of the page to see the links.) The expected behavior is that clicking each link should alert "This is link 0" or "This is link 5" depending on the link. But if you try it, every link alerts "This is link 10." Why is that?

This function is lexically scoped to the i variable:

```
link.onclick = function() {
    alert("This is link " + i);
    return false;
};
```

When it runs, it accesses the current value of i. Since the for loop finished executing long before you clicked the link, the value of i is 10, the final value of the loop. To fix this, you need to create a new scope to hold the value of i for each onclick function.

```
for (var i = 0; i < 10; i++) {
    var link = document.createElement("a");
    link.innerHTML = "Link " + i;
    link.href = "#";
```

```
    link.onclick = (function(num) {
        // The value of onclick will be
        // this anonymous function
        return function() {
            alert("This is link " + num);
            return false;
        };
    }(i); // Pass i to the self-invoking function
    document.body.appendChild(link);
}
```

This code works as expected, because the num variable in each onclick function is set to the value of i at that point in the loop.

One final practical example shows how you can permanently bind the context of a function using closures and apply(). Start with the following example (from the earlier "Functions as Methods" section):

```
var myObject = {
    someProperty: 42
};
myObject.method = function() {
    console.log(this.someProperty);
};

var objectMethod = myObject.method;
objectMethod();
undefined
```

Here is the function that binds a function's context:

```
function bindContext(func, context) {
    return function() {
```

(continues on next page)

```
        return func.apply(context, arguments);
    };
}

var boundMethod = bindContext(myObject.method, myObject);
boundMethod();
42
```

The boundMethod variable holds the return value of bindContext(), which is another function. This inner function retains access to the func and context arguments passed to bindContext(). When the function on boundMethod executes, it calls func in the proper context using the apply() method.

Recursion

Recursion is when a function calls itself. This is often useful in mathematics, such as finding the *nth* number in the Fibonacci series (1, 2, 3, 5, 8, 13, 21...).

```
function fibonacci(n) {
    if ( n < 2 ) {
        return 1;
    } else {
        return fibonacci(n-2) + fibonacci(n-1);
    }
}
fibonacci(5);
8
fibonacci(10);
89
```

The fibonacci() function calls itself with a different value for n until n reaches 1 or less. Recursive functions always need a stopping point, or they will continue to recurse until the browser stops the script and displays a warning to the user.

Caching

If you write a function that you call repeatedly, it might be smart to store the results so that successive calls are faster. This is called *caching*. Here's an example that speeds up repeated calls to the previously shown fibonnaci() function:

```
var fibonacci = (function() {
    // The inner function will retain access
    // to this cache object
    var cache = {};

    return function(n) {
        // If we've already solved for this value of n
        // it will be stored in the cache, so we
        // can return it
        if (cache[n]) {
            return cache[n];
        }

        // This demonstrates that the caching works
        console.log("solving for " + n);

        // Store the value in a variable so
        // we can cache it before returning it
        if ( n < 2 ) {
```

(continues on next page)

```
            var result = 1;
        } else {
            var result = fibonacci(n-2) + fibonacci(n-1);
        }

        // Caching the result based on the argument
        cache[n] = result;
        return result;
    }
})(); // Self-invoking function executes automatically

fibonacci(5);
solving for 5
solving for 3
solving for 1
solving for 2
solving for 0
solving for 4
8
fibonacci(6); // 0-5 are already solved for
solving for 6
13
```

When you call fibonacci(5) the first time, it recursively calls itself multiple times to determine the result. But since the result is cached, each successive call does far less work.

Memoization

Memoization is a technique similar to caching that takes advantage of the fact that functions are just data. Once an expensive function runs, it can rewrite itself with an optimized version.

```
var getElement = function() {
    console.log("creating element");
    var element = document.createElement("div");
    // ... Do a bunch of expensive operations

    // Overwrite the function with a simpler version
    getElement = function() {
        return element;
    };
    return element;
};
```

The first time getElement runs, it creates the element and runs a bunch of code with it. Then it rewrites the getElement function to solely return the created element. This makes subsequent calls to getElement much quicker.

6

Objects

Understanding objects is crucial to writing well-organized, expressive JavaScript. If you've used other languages such as Java or ActionScript, JavaScript may seem like it's missing a lot of language features such as classes and modules. But objects in JavaScript are flexible and powerful enough that you don't often miss those features. Sometimes you can even emulate missing language features with clever uses of objects and functions.

Basics

The best way to create an object is to use an object literal.

```
var myObject = {};
```

You can create an object with properties by listing them in the object literal, separating property names and values with colons.

```
var myObject = {
    propertyName : "most names are valid identifiers",
    "arbitrary strings" : "can be property names too",
    42 : "property names can be numbers"
};
```

> **tip** Notice that each property: value pair is separated by a comma, but make sure not to put a comma after the last pair. Most browsers ignore it, but Internet Explorer throws a hard-to-find error.

Properties can be any value, including objects and functions.

You can access a property value by its name in two ways: with the dot operator (.) or with the bracket operator ([]). These two expressions are identical:

```
myObject.property1 = 42;
myObject["property1"] = 42;
```

To use the dot operator, the property name must be a valid identifier. The bracket operator takes an expression and uses its value as the property name. The following would not work because in this case property1 is an undefined variable:

```
myObject[property1] = 42;
ReferenceError: property1 is not defined
```

But if you had already declared the variable property1 to have a value, that value would work as a property name.

```
// Variable holding the property name
var property1 = "propertyName";
myObject[property1] = 42;
// The actual name of the property
myObject.propertyName;
42
```

The bracket operator is very flexible. With it, you can use any value as a property name, even other objects.

```
mySecondObject = {};
mySecondObject[myObject] = 108;
```

You can even call methods using the bracket syntax and the string version of the method name.

```
var myArray = [1,2,3];
myArray["push"](4, 5);
[1, 2, 3, 4, 5]
```

Most JavaScript coders prefer the dot operator because it uses fewer keystrokes unless they need the flexibility of the bracket operator.

Looping Over Properties

You can loop over all of the *enumerable* properties of an object with the for/in statement.

```
var myObject = {
    property1: 42,
    property2: "string value",
    property3: true
};                                          (continues on next page)
```

```javascript
for (var propertyName in myObject) {
   // Print out the name of the property
   console.log("name: " + propertyName);

   // Print out the property value
   var value = myObject[propertyName];
   console.log("value: " + value);
}
"name: property1"
"value: 42"
"name: property2"
"value: string value"
"name: property3"
"value: true"
```

In each loop of the for/in statement, you get a variable holding the name of a property. You can then access the property value using the bracket operator.

You can loop over any object with the for/in statement, including arrays.

```javascript
var myArray = ["a", "b", "c"];

for (var propertyName in myArray) {
   // The property name is its index
   console.log(propertyName);

   var value = myArray[propertyName];
   console.log(value);
}
0
"a"
1
```

```
"b"
2
"c"
```

Enumerable Properties

Remember that all those array methods such as push() and slice() are properties of arrays too. But they don't show up when you loop over the properties of myArray. This is because they are not *enumerable*. All objects have a convenience function called propertyIsEnumerable() to check this:

```
var myArray = [1,2,3];
myArray.propertyIsEnumerable(0);
true
myArray.propertyIsEnumerable("push");
false
```

I've never had a reason to use propertyIsEnumerable() in my code, but it helps explain the reasons for using hasOwnProperty().

Using prototypes, which I'll explain in the "Prototypes" section later in this chapter, you can add properties to every single object at the same time.

```
Object.prototype.someRandomProperty = 42;
{}.someRandomProperty;
42
[].someRandomProperty;
42
"".someRandomProperty;
42
```

When you add a property to an object or an object's prototype, it is always enumerable. This is unlike built-in properties such as push() or toString(). Your added properties will show up in every for/in loop.

```
Object.prototype.someRandomProperty = 42;
var myArray = [1,2,3];
for (var propertyName in myArray) {
    console.log(myArray[propertyName]);
}
1
2
3
42
```

To protect yourself from unexpectedly looping over these properties, *always* use the hasOwnProperty() method to test whether the property belongs only to that object.

```
for (var propertyName in myArray) {
    // This filters out someRandomProperty
    if (myArray.hasOwnProperty(propertyName)) {
        console.log(myArray[propertyName]);
    }
}
1
2
3
```

tip

When using arrays, it's always best practice to use for **and** while **loops because you can be sure that the** i **variable is an integer.**

It's tempting to skip using hasOwnProperty(), especially if you are careful not to add properties to any built-in prototypes. But keep in mind that any script in the page can alter built-in objects. It's not just your code that you have to be careful of.

Deleting Properties

You can remove properties from an object by using the delete operator. The property will no longer show up in a for/in loop. The delete operator returns true only if it could successfully delete the property.

```
var myObject = {
    property1 : 42,
    property2 : 108
};

for (var propertyName in myObject) {
    console.log(propertyName, myObject[propertyName]);
}
property1 42
property2 108

// This deletes the property completely
delete myObject.property1;
true

myObject.property1;
undefined

// This just changes the value of the property
// instead of removing it
myObject.property2 = null;

for (var propertyName in myObject) {
```
(continues on next page)

```
    console.log(propertyName, myObject[propertyName]);
}
property2 null
```

Constructor Functions

All data types, even primitives such as Number and String, have *constructor functions*. They are rarely used because literals are faster and easier.

```
new Number(5);
5
new String("hello");
"hello"
new Boolean();
true
```

You also don't want to use them because checking the data type gets confusing.

```
typeof new Number(5);
"object"
typeof new Number(5).valueOf();
"number"
```

I only point this out because you can create your own data types with constructor functions, which are normal functions called right after the new keyword.

```
var MyDataType = function() {

};
var myData = new MyDataType();
```

Constructor functions are one of the rare places where it's customary to start the name with a capital letter. It tells you that it's meant to be used with the new keyword.

Inside the constructor function, you can use the this keyword to add properties to new *instances* of the data type. This is a great way to create reusable pieces of code.

```
var Jedi = function(name) {
    this.name = name;
    this.theForce = "strong";
};

var obiwan = new Jedi("Obi Wan");
var yoda = new Jedi("Yoda");

yoda.name;
"Yoda"
Yoda.theForce;
"strong"
obiwan.theForce;
"strong"
```

Prototypes

All arrays have the same methods, like push(), slice(), and join(). All strings have split(), substr(), and replace(). And every object has the toString() method. Where do these methods come from?

It turns out that every data type has a prototype object that defines a set of properties. Each instance of a data type has access to the properties of its type's prototype.

You can find the prototype object for a type by accessing the prototype property on its constructor function, like this:

```
Number.prototype;
String.prototype;
Array.prototype;
Object.prototype;
```

When you access a property of an object, JavaScript follows these steps to find the value of that property:

1. First, it looks for the property on the object. When you add the property directly to the object, JavaScript finds the value here.

   ```
   var myArray = [1,2,3];
   myArray[0];
   1
   ```

2. If the property doesn't exist on the object, JavaScript looks at the prototype of the object's constructor.

   ```
   myArray.push;
   push()
   Array.prototype.push;
   push()
   myArray.push === Array.prototype.push;
   true
   ```

3. You can tell that push() exists on Array.prototype and not on myArray with the hasOwnProperty() method.

   ```
   myArray.hasOwnProperty("push");
   false
   ```

4. Finally, if the property can't be found on the object or the prototype of the object's constructor, JavaScript determines that it doesn't exist. If you try to call it as a method, you'll get an error.

```
typeof myArray.missingProperty;
"undefined"
myArray.missingProperty();
TypeError: myArray.missingProperty is not a function
```

Changing Built-in Prototypes

You can add, change, and remove properties from the prototypes of built-in types. I'll get to why this can be a bad idea in a moment, but first I'll show some examples.

In Chapter 4, you learned how to trim spaces off the beginnings and endings of a string. That function works like this:

```
stringTrim("  hello  ");
"hello"
```

You can turn that function into a method for every string by adding it to String.prototype.

```
String.prototype.trim = function() {
    // Since this is a method, the context is the string
    // that you can access with the "this" keyword
    return this.replace(/^(\s|\u00A0)+|(\s|\u00A0)+$/g, "");
};

"  hello  ".trim();
"hello"
"  this string also has the trim method  ".trim();
"this string also has the trim method"
```

In my opinion, this is often a much more pleasant way to organize code. It is sometimes referred to as an *object-oriented* style of programming, because you act upon objects with methods. (The stringTrim() style is *functional* programming because you're passing values to functions.)

Adding Modern JavaScript to Older Browsers

Functions such as `string.trim()` are part of the ECMAScript specification, but they aren't supported in most browsers yet. Adding them to the built-in prototypes yourself is a good way to take advantage of new additions to the language. However, you should check to see whether the browser supports a function before adding it because the built-in version is always faster.

```
if (! String.prototype.trim) {
    // The browser doesn't support string.trim(),
    // so you can add it here
    String.prototype.trim = function() {
        // ...
    }
}
```

Potential Problems with prototype

You have to be careful when changing built-in prototypes, because you're basically creating your own version of JavaScript. If you're using code written by someone else, such as a JavaScript library or an advertisement service, you might change some JavaScript objects that they rely on.

Also, every property you create is enumerable, so each one will show up in `for/in` loops. This is most problematic if you change `Object.prototype` since it will affect every object created. Always avoid changing `Object.prototype`, and use caution when changing any other built-in prototype.

Prototypes for Custom Data Types

Your custom data types can have prototypes too. This is the best way to add common properties and methods to all the instances of your data type.

```
var Jedi = function(name) {
    this.name = name;
};

Jedi.prototype = {
    theForce: "strong",
    lightSaber: function() {
        console.log("Shrruumm! Shr-zzmm!");
    }
};

var obiwan = new Jedi("Obi Wan");
var yoda = new Jedi("Yoda");
```

You can access the properties from the Jedi prototype like any other property.

```
yoda.theForce;
"strong"
yoda.lightSaber();
"Shrruumm! Shr-zzmm!"
```

All Jedis share the properties of their prototype object.

```
obiwan.lightSaber();
"Shrruumm! Shr-zzmm!"
```

You can still add properties to individual objects that don't affect any of the others.

```
obiwan.saberColor = "blue";
"blue"
```

Changing the prototype affects all instances of the data type regardless of when they were created.

```
Jedi.prototype.mindTrick = function() {
    console.log("Waves hand");
};

yoda.mindTrick();
"Waves hand"
obiwan.mindTrick();
"Waves hand"
```

How to Understand Constructor Functions and Prototypes

The new keyword and object prototypes may look like somewhat magical behavior, but they're actually pretty simple. The following code is a simplistic example, but it should give you a sense of what's going on under the hood.

```
var ConstructorFunc = function() {
    // Act on "this", which is the
    // new instance of this data type
    // These override the properties
    // on the prototype
    this.description = "I'm an instance of ConstructorFunc";
};
```

```
ConstructorFunc.prototype = {
    property : 42,
    method : function() {
        alert(this.description);
    }
};

// Instead of using the new keyword, create the
// new object yourself
var instance = {};
// Then assign the properties of the prototype to
// the instance
for (var name in ConstructorFunc.prototype) {
    instance[name] = ConstructorFunc.prototype[name];
}
// Finally, call the constructor function in the context
// of the object
ConstructorFunc.call(instance);

instance.method();
```

The browser will show an alert dialog saying "I'm an instance of ConstructorFunc."

Now you've manually created an instance of the ConstructorFunc data type. Of course, it's a lot quicker to just use new ConstructorFunc(). Also, properties on a data type's prototype object won't show up when using hasOwnProperty(). In my simplistic example, I'm adding the properties directly to the object, so they will appear in any for/in loops.

Object-Oriented Patterns

You may already be familiar with an object-oriented language such as Java, PHP, or ActionScript 3 that includes concepts like modules and classes. JavaScript doesn't have these concepts built into the language, but it is flexible enough that you can simulate them with custom data types and prototypes. You can even simulate inheritance.

Inheritance is a way of modeling your data with general data types that have common functionality and specific data types that have specific functionality. Start with a general data type, as shown here:

```
var Person = function(name) {
    this.name = name;
};

Person.prototype = {
    says : function(message) {
        console.log(this.name + " says " + message);
    }
};

var lenny = new Person("Lenny");
lenny.says("Hello!");
"Lenny says Hello!"
```

Now you can make a more specific type of person, but it should still have the same name attribute, as well as the says() method.

```
var Jedi = function(name, saberColor) {
    Person.call(this, name);
    this.saberColor = saberColor;
};
```

`Person.call(this, name)` lets you reuse the `Person()` constructor function to change instances of this new data type. Then you can make it more specific by using the new `saberColor` argument.

```
Jedi.prototype = new Person();
```

You assign a person object as the Jedi `prototype` so that the Jedi objects share properties and methods of People objects.

```
Jedi.prototype.lightSaber = function() {
    console.log("Shrruumm! Shr-zzmm!");
};
```

Now you can add new properties and methods to the Jedi data type that don't exist on the Person data type.

```
var yoda = new Jedi("Yoda", "blue");
var macewindu = new Jedi("Mace Windu", "purple");

yoda.says("Do or do not, there is no try.");
"Yoda says Do or do not, there is no try."
```

Instances of the Jedi data type share the methods and properties of the Person data type, so you can still use the `says()` method on the `yoda` object.

```
macewindu.lightSaber();
"Shrruumm! Shr-zzmm!"
```

These instances have new methods to use that are specific to the Jedi data type.

You can use the `instanceof` operator to determine the type of an object.

```
lenny instanceof Person;
true
```

(continues on next page)

```
lenny instanceof Jedi;
false
yoda instanceof Person;
true
yoda instanceof Jedi;
true
```

Since Jedi inherits from Person, yoda is an instance of both data types.

Inheritance is the reason why all objects have methods like toString()
and hasOwnProperty(). All data types inherit from Object.

```
lenny instanceof Object;
true
myArray instanceof Object;
true
```

Namespacing

Namespacing is a common technique for keeping code separate and
reducing naming conflicts. In JavaScript, all you need to do is create
objects that store your code and data away from other objects. Often,
you name these objects after your Web sites because URLs are guaran-
teed to be unique. Also, URLs use periods, which look a whole lot like
JavaScript dot operators.

note Many other languages provide special language features to support
namespacing. JavaScript lacks these features, but objects are flexible
enough to get some of the benefits of namespacing to better organize your code.

```
var PEACHPIT = {};
PEACHPIT.com = {};
PEACHPIT.com.sayHello = function() {
```

```
    console.log("Hello!");
};
```

Naming your top object in all capitals indicates to yourself and others to be careful never to reassign that variable.

The reason for namespacing is that you may want to use a script on your pages that defines its own sayHello() function. Because these functions are namespaced, there's little chance for them to overwrite each other.

```
var HURLEYS_SCRIPTS = {};
HURLEYS_SCRIPTS.com = {};
HURLEYS_SCRIPTS.com.sayHello = function() {
    console.log("Hey dude!");
};
```

You may have a second script with a different sayHello() function, but you still want to put it in the same PEACHPIT namespace. You can add another object to the namespace, but make sure not to overwrite any of your namespace objects.

```
// Conditional variable assignment with OR (||)
var PEACHPIT = PEACHPIT || {};
PEACHPIT.com = PEACHPIT.com || {};
PEACHPIT.com.helperFunctions =
➥ PEACHPIT.com.helperFunctions || {};
PEACHPIT.com.helperFunctions.sayHello = function() {
    console.log("Hello again!");
};
```

You can use conditional assignment to ensure that your namespace objects exist or create new objects if they don't. This uses the same pattern as assigning default values to arguments that you saw in Chapter 5.

Local References

Of course, you definitely don't want to type
PEACHPIT.com.helperFunctions.sayHello() every time you want to
use this function. Fortunately, you don't have to if you put all your code
inside of a function like this:

```
(function() {
    // Save a local reference to your namespace objects
    // for quick access
    var P = window.PEACHPIT;
    var helpers = P.com.helperFunctions;

    helpers.sayHello();

    // ... Declare any other functions and variables
    // here. They will be scoped inside this function
    // so there's no chance of another script causing
    // any conflicts
})(); // Self-invoking function executes automatically
```

The Global Object

In Chapter 5, you learned that all functions execute in a context that you can refer to with the this keyword. A simple function executed normally runs in the global context. In a browser, the global object is window.

```
function myFunc() {
    console.log(this);
}
myFunc();
Window
```

When you learned about variable scope in Chapter 5, you learned that variables outside of functions are in the *global scope*. In fact, declaring a variable in the global scope is the same as making a property on the global object.

```
var globalVar = 42;
window.globalVar;
42
```

In Chapter 2, you learned about a few global functions such as isNaN()
and parseInt(). These functions are also properties of the global object.

```
window.isNaN("1a");
true
window.parseInt("1a");
1
```

The global object is obviously a very important object, but I left it until
this chapter for two reasons: You can write plenty of JavaScript without
ever realizing that it's there, and it's the first object you'll learn about
when you learn to write JavaScript for the browser in Chapter 9. The
following are a few details about the global object before you dive into
programming Web pages.

Global Variables

Global variables are variables declared outside any function scope.

```
var myGlobalVariable = 42;
```

The fact that global variables are properties of the window object gives
you more flexibility and specificity when using global variables inside
functions.

```
var myVar = "global variable";

function myFunc() {
   var myVar = "scoped variable";
```

```
    console.log(myVar);
    console.log(window.myVar);
}

myFunc();
"scoped variable"
"global variable"
```

In the previous code, because you declared a second myVar variable inside myFunc, you can't access the global myVar variable just by name. But you still have access to the window object, so you can access the global variable as a property on myVar.

Functions declarations work the same way.

```
function myGlobalFunction() {

}
typeof window.myGlobalFunction;
"function"
```

Accidentally Creating Global Variables

If you forget to use the var keyword when declaring a variable inside a function, it becomes a global variable reference.

```
(function() {
    // Forgot the var keyword
    myLocalVar = "whoops it's global!";
})(); // Self-invoking function executes automatically
console.log(myLocalVar);
"whoops it's global!"
```

Global Variable Best Practices

You should limit your global variables and functions as much as possible. Another script could easily overwrite your global variables and cause hard-to-find bugs in your code. Fortunately, you can take advantage of function scope to control access to your variables and functions.

For simple scripts, I like to put all my code inside a self-invoking function. For more complicated scripts, especially ones that interact with other scripts, I prefer storing all the code on a single namespace object. See Chapters 5 and 6 for examples of both these techniques.

Global Functions

Core JavaScript doesn't provide too many global functions. Most functions are methods on built-in object types. You already learned about a few useful ones for numbers and strings such as parseInt() and encodeURIComponent().

Timers

Browsers execute JavaScript code line by line as quickly as possible, but sometimes you need to introduce a delay before executing some code.

setTimeout(func, delay)

The setTimeout() function delays the execution of a function until at least delay milliseconds.

JavaScript is *single-threaded*, meaning it can execute only a single instruction at a time. If the browser is already doing something by the time delay rolls around, it waits until the thread is free. (By "instruction," I mean any statements, expressions, events, or other pieces of code that the browser executes. All instructions take a finite amount of time to execute, even if it's only a few milliseconds.)

If you pass in zero milliseconds for delay, it executes func with the shortest delay possible.

The return value of setTimeout() is an identifier for use with clearTimeout().

```
function callback() {
    console.log("At least three seconds passed");
}

setTimeout(callback, 3000);
```

The console will output the following after a short delay:

```
"At least three seconds passed"
```

setInterval(func, delay)

The setInterval() function repeats the execution of a function at least every delay milliseconds. It also returns an identifier to use with clearInterval().

Unlike setTimeout(), you must pass a delay of more than zero milliseconds.

```
setInterval(callback, 3000);
```

Roughly every three seconds, the console displays "At least three seconds passed" until you unload the page.

If the browser is busy with another instruction when interval comes up, setInterval() waits until the browser is free to execute the callback function. Just like setTimeout(), you can't rely on setInterval() to execute the callback after an exact period of time.

clearInterval(id), clearTimeout(id)

If you need to stop a callback function from executing, you must store the identifier returned by setTimeout() or setInterval() and pass it to either of these two functions.

By clearing a timeout, you can stop the callback function from ever executing. Here's a good way to make nothing happen:

```
var timeoutId = setTimeout(callback, 3000);
clearTimeout(timeoutId);
```

In this example, the callback function keeps track of how many times it gets called and clears the interval after five calls.

```
function fiveTimes() {
    console.log("Interval " + fiveTimes.count);
    // Add 1 to count and compare it to 5. If
    // over 5, stop the interval
    if (++fiveTimes.count > 5) {
        clearInterval(intervalId);
    }
}
fiveTimes.count = 1;

var intervalId = setInterval(fiveTimes, 3000);
```

The console will count up to 5 before clearing the interval and stopping.

Asynchronous Programming

The setTimeout() and setInterval() functions are the first examples in this book of *asynchronous programming*. You'll also encounter
this crucial JavaScript concept when you learn about events, Ajax,
and animation in Chapters 11, 15, and 16, respectively.

A script is asynchronous when code can be executed at arbitrary
points in time. JavaScript embraces this concept by treating functions as just another type of data. You can pass around functions as
callbacks and event handlers, not knowing exactly when (if ever) the
browser will call them. You may want a function to run when the
user clicks the mouse, but you can't know when they will actually
do so.

Asynchronous programming makes function context binding much
more complicated. Consider this example:

```
var myObject = {
    value : "myObject's value",
    method : function() {
        console.log(this.value);
    }
};

setTimeout(myObject.method, 3000);
```

The method function executes about three seconds later, but it's no
longer bound to myObject. Without that context, this.value returns
undefined.   *(continues on next page)*

Asynchronous Programming (continued)

The most common solution is to create an anonymous function that calls the function in the context of myObject.

```
setTimeout(function() {
    myObject.method();
}, 3000);
```

You could also use the bindContext() function from Chapter 6.

```
setTimeout(bindContext(myObject.method, myObject), 3000);
```

You may also want to pass arguments to the callback function. Anonymous functions are also useful in this case:

```
setTimeout(function() {
    callbackFunction("an argument");
}, 3000);
```

Keep these techniques in mind when working with events and other code that involves indeterminate delays in execution.

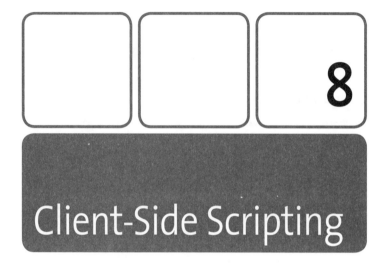

8

Client-Side Scripting

Up until now, I really haven't covered any practical uses of JavaScript. You can go only so far manipulating simple data such as strings and arrays. JavaScript is a "scripting language," which by definition operates inside some kind of environment. Usually, this environment is an HTML document in a Web browser. From here on, this book focuses on interacting with browsers, Web pages, servers, and user input.

Script Tags

HTML provides a means of including executable code in the form of the `<script>` element. You can include code in a Web page in two ways.

Inline Scripts

Inline scripts include JavaScript code directly in the markup, like this:

```
<script type="text/javascript">
   var element = document.getElementById("domId");
</script>
```

Inline scripts allow you to include your code as text right in the Web page. This is great for quickly testing a solution or adding code that is specific to this particular page.

Remote Scripts

Remote scripts instruct the browser to download a separate script file and execute it in the page. The `src` attribute points to the script file like any other URL.

```
<script src="my-script.js" type="text/javascript"></script>
```

In most cases, this is the preferred solution for a few reasons:

- Storing JavaScript directly in HTML with an inline script makes your HTML files larger and harder to maintain.

- You can easily include the same script in multiple pages just by including the same remote `<script>` tag.

- Browsers cache JavaScript files so they don't have to download a script file twice when visiting another page that uses it.

Where to Include the <script> Tag

You can use the <script> tag nearly anywhere in an HTML document. I recommend including inline and remote scripts at the very end, right before the closing </body> tag. This has two advantages:

- When some browsers encounter a <script> tag, they halt any other processes until they download and parse the script. By including scripts at the end, you allow the browser to download and render all page elements, style sheets, and images without any unnecessary delays.

- Since the browser encounters and renders the Web page before executing any script, you know that all page elements are already available for you to retrieve and manipulate.

Putting <script> tags at the end has one distinct disadvantage, however. Because the Web page downloads and renders first, there may be a noticeable delay before any scripts execute. This should not be the case with the short examples in this book, so I will use this general template for HTML documents:

```
<!DOCTYPE html>
<html>
    <head>
        <title></title>
        <link rel="stylesheet" href="styles.css"
➥ type="text/css" />
    </head>
    <body>
        <!-- page elements go here -->
        <script src="my-script.js" type="text/javascript">
➥ </script>
    </body>
</html>
```

Nonblocking and Lazy Loading

What I'll show next is an advanced technique, but you'll encounter it in later chapters that use certain JavaScript libraries, so I'll briefly explain it here.

You can use JavaScript to include other script files in a Web page. You simply create a `<script>` element and append it to the document.

```
var script = document.createElement("script");
script.type = "text/javascript";
script.src = "my-script.js";
document.getElementsByTagName("head")[0].appendChild(script);
```

When you dynamically append a script to a page, the browser does not halt other processes, so it continues rendering page elements and downloading resources. This is called *nonblocking* script loading.

You can also use this technique at arbitrary times in your script. You may decide to include only a small amount of code at page load and then download other script files only when needed. This is called *lazy loading*.

Many popular JavaScript libraries now include utility functions to encourage these practices. Some libraries exist specifically for this purpose, such as LABjs (*http://labjs.com/*). Other libraries use it as the primary method of including scripts in a page, such as YUI 3 (*http://developer.yahoo.com/yui/3/*).

Unless they use a library that leverages nonblocking script loading, the examples in this book will use simple `<script>` elements to include JavaScript in HTML.

The Browser Problem

Programming in pure JavaScript is relatively straightforward, but once you add the myriad of browsers available to the equation, everything gets significantly more complicated.

Brandon Eich developed JavaScript for Netscape 2.0 in the midst of the "browser wars" of the late 1990s. To keep up, Microsoft made its own version of JavaScript that it called JScript. It wasn't an exact copy of the original implementation, and many of the original differences persist today.

In addition, the Web and its technologies continue to evolve at a rapid pace. Browser makers have the daunting task of innovating their products and keeping up with each other, all while maintaining backward compatibility with the billions of Web sites that exist on the Internet.

Fortunately, groups such as the W3C, WHATWG, and ECMA have made great strides in codifying and standardizing JavaScript and browser APIs. Their efforts allow developers to more easily "write once, run anywhere" and trust that their code will continue to work as the Web evolves. Most modern browsers, such as Firefox, Safari, Opera, and Chrome, follow Web standards very closely. Internet Explorer still lags behind in standards support and is often a thorn in every developer's side.

JavaScript developers tackle browser differences with libraries of code that help provide consistent APIs across all browsers. You'll learn about libraries soon, but the next few chapters focus on pure JavaScript objects, properties, and functions.

What Does API Mean?

API stands for *application programming interface*, which is a somewhat generic term for whatever tools you use to programmatically interact with a piece of software. Browser APIs are mostly functions and properties that give you access to browser windows, elements in HTML documents, and even certain parts of the user's computer.

Progressive Enhancement

Web development is an interesting and challenging field because you can't reliably know how the user will end up viewing your code.

Usually, the ideal end user is someone using a modern browser on a fast computer with a high-speed Internet connection. This may describe the majority of Web surfers, but dozens of factors affect how any given person might see your code:

- Some people can't or won't upgrade from an older browser.

- Some people have slower computers with smaller screens.

- Some people surf the Web on mobile devices with tiny screens and no mice.

- Some people don't have fine motor control, so computer mice aren't a viable option.

- Some people are visually impaired and use *screen reader* software to operate computers using aural cues.

- Some people lock down their browsers out of a concern for privacy, so JavaScript and cookies aren't available.

Creating interesting, engaging, and useful Web pages that anyone can use is a daunting challenge, but it is possible. The most prevalent strategy is commonly known as *progressive enhancement*.

I like to think of Web development as layers upon layers (**Figure 10.1**). HTML is your most basic, fundamental layer. A well-organized HTML page should be accessible to any user because it is just plain text decorated with a bit of meaning (or *semantics*) using HTML tags.

Figure 8.1
The layers of Web development.

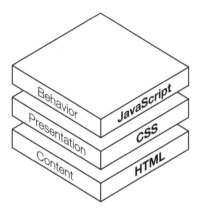

CSS is your second layer, which determines presentation and layout. Some users, especially the visually impaired, won't get this layer.

JavaScript is your third layer, which adds behavior and interactivity. The number of users without JavaScript is dwindling, but they still exist.

Images, plug-ins such as Flash and Silverlight, video, and audio are examples of additional layers of Web content.

Because it's inherently the most accessible, the fundamental HTML layer should be the only layer required to use your Web pages. Each layer above that should just *progressively enhance* the content below it, making the experience more attractive, more efficient, and more engaging. If a layer isn't available to a user, the core content of the page should still be just as accessible.

One of your most important "users" isn't a person at all. Search engine robots are like blind, deaf, keyboard-reliant users who browse the Web with images and JavaScript turned off. Search engine optimization (SEO) and progressive enhancement often go hand in hand.

Progressive enhancement and accessibility are incredibly important topics that unfortunately are a bit beyond the scope of this book. Still, I'll show how I include progressive enhancement techniques in my examples starting in Chapter 14 of the book.

Handling Non-JavaScript Situations

If a user comes to your page without JavaScript, you can use two different techniques to make sure your content is still accessible. Keep in mind that your HTML and CSS foundation must be well organized for these techniques to be of any use.

The <noscript> Tag

Browsers only show the content inside the <noscript> tags when JavaScript is unavailable. I don't find this to be terribly useful; it's often used to display a message notifying the user of the missing JavaScript behaviors.

```
<noscript>
    <p>This page requires JavaScript.</p>
</noscript>
```

Requiring JavaScript goes against the principles of progressive enhancement, so I avoid code like this whenever I can.

JavaScript-Specific CSS Classes

I use the following technique a lot so that I can write CSS for situations with and without JavaScript by replacing the no-js class with the js class. Start by including a no-js class in your markup, as shown here:

```
<html class="no-js">
```

Then include a <script> tag that immediately replaces that class with a js class.

```
<script type="text/javascript">
    document.documentElement.className = document.
➡ documentElement.className.replace(/\bno-js\b/, "js");
</script>
```

I like this technique enough, in fact, that I prefer a shorter version, as shown here:

```
(function(d, c) {
    d[c] = d[c].replace(/\bno-js\b/, "js");
})(document.documentElement, "className");
```

By passing in the repetitive parts of that line of code as the arguments of a self-invoking function, I can reference them as single-character variable names (document.documentElement becomes d, and "className" becomes c).

This is one of the rare times when I want to include a <script> tag earlier in the page, such as in the <head> element. Replacing the no-js class as quickly as possible reduces any flashes of content as the page loads.

Using this technique gives me the freedom to write CSS rules like this:

```
html.no-js .accessibilityMessage {
    display: block
}

html.js #alternateNav {
    display: none;
}
```

note
Credit for this technique goes to Paul Irish (*http://paulirish.com/*).

Browsers and Windows

You learned in previous chapters that window is the global object in client-side JavaScript. Many of its properties and methods are part of the core JavaScript language, but it also has many other that are specific to programming in the browser. This chapter gives a quick overview and reference of the properties and methods that directly relate to browsers and browser windows.

Properties

Browser windows have a couple of properties that mostly deal with the size and position of the window on the screen. These properties are read-only, and you'll need to use the `window` methods described in the next sections to change their values.

- **innerHeight**, **innerWidth** Represent the pixel values of the size of the browser viewport. The *viewport* is the scrollable area inside the window. The following are the equivalent properties for most versions of Internet Explorer:

```
document.documentElement.clientHeight;
document.documentElement.clientWidth;
```

- **outerHeight**, **outerWidth** Represent the pixel values of the size of the browser window. Internet Explorer does not have equivalent properties.

- **pageXOffset**, **pageYOffset** Represent the pixel values for how far the user has scrolled the page. The following are the equivalent properties for most versions of Internet Explorer:

```
document.documentElement.scrollLeft;
document.documentElement.scrollTop;
```

- **screenLeft**, **screenTop**, **screenX**, **screenY** Represent the position of the browser window on the user's screen. There is little agreement between browsers about which property to use, so you must check both.

```
var screenX = window.screenX || window.screenLeft;
var screenY = window.screenY || window.screenTop;
```

Coordinates on the Screen

Most people are used to coordinate systems that start in the bottom right. The X value moves the left as it gets bigger, and the Y value moves up as it gets bigger. On computer screens, the Y value gets flipped (**Figure 9.1**).

Figure 9.1

The screen coordinate system.

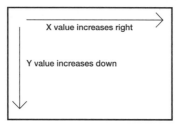

X value increases right

Y value increases down

Global Functions

Advertisers and spammers have abused some of these methods, especially window.open(), which they use to create pop-up and pop-under windows. Use discretion when manipulating browser windows to avoid obnoxious and intrusive behavior.

Dialog Boxes

Dialog boxes allow for rudimentary user interaction. I don't like using them unless I really need to demand the user's attention. They are *modal*, which means the user must dismiss the dialog box before being allowed to interact with the rest of the browser again.

- **alert(message)** Show a dialog with the message and an OK button. `alert()` is useful for debugging in browsers such as Internet Explorer 6 that don't have `console.log()`. Objects passed to `alert()` are coerced into a string via the `toString()` method, which often only returns `"[object Object]"`, so it's not nearly as useful as a real console.

- **confirm(message)** Shows a dialog box that includes Cancel and OK buttons. The method returns `true` or `false` based on whether the user clicked OK or Cancel, respectively. Be very careful when using this method because it's often difficult to write questions that can really be answered by Cancel or OK.

- **prompt(message[, *defaultResponse*])** Shows a dialog box that includes a text field for the user to enter a response string. The field is prepopulated with `defaultResponse` if provided.

Manipulating Browser Windows

You have some control over browser windows, but again, try not to annoy or frustrate your users with these methods.

- **open(url, name[, *features*])** Opens the page located at `url` in a new window, or if a window with the name `name` already exists, the `url` opens in that window. It returns a reference to the opened window that you can control programmatically.

  The `features` argument is an optional string specifying what browser features the new window should have. It is a comma-separated list of `"feature=value"` pairs. Most values are "yes" or "no" except for `height` and `width`, which expect pixel values.

  Some browsers like Firefox ignore "no" values on the location bar to make it harder to pretend to be a secure site like a banking website.

```
var newWindow = open("http://www.google.com",
➥"searchWindow", "location=yes,menubar=yes,
➥resizable=yes,scrollbars=yes,status=yes,
➥toolbar=yes,width=600,height=400,left=10,top=10");
```

- **close()** Closes a window that you opened programmatically. You cannot close a window that you didn't open, including the current window.

- **moveBy(deltaX, deltaY)** Moves the window a certain number of pixels from the current position. The arguments can be negative or positive integers. A positive deltaX moves the window to the right, and a negative deltaY moves the window up.

- **moveTo(x, y)** Moves the window to the x, y position on the user's screen.

- **resizeBy(deltaWidth, deltaHeight)** Resizes a window a certain number of pixels from the current size. The arguments can be positive or negative integers. Calling resizeBy(50, -25) on a window that is 600x800 pixels results in a 650x775 pixel window.

- **resizeTo(width, height)** Resizes a window to be width pixels wide and height pixels tall. Browsers no longer allow you to resize a window to be very small so that you can't hide a window from a user. This applies to resizeBy() as well.

- **scrollBy(deltaX, deltaY)** Scrolls the document to the left by deltaX pixels and down by deltaY pixels.

- **scrollTo(x, y)** Scrolls the document so that the part of the document located at x, y is in the top-left corner of the browser viewport.

- **focus()** Brings a browser window to the front and sets it to respond to keyboard events.

- **blur()** The opposite of focus(), sending the window behind other windows so that it won't respond to keyboard events.

- **print()** Brings up the browser's Print dialog box.

The history Object

The history object gives you programmatic access to the browser's Back and Forward buttons. It has three methods: back(), forward(), and go().

```
// Same as pressing the Back button
window.history.back();
// Same as pressing the Forward button
window.history.forward();
// Same pressing the Back button twice
window.history.go(-2);
// Same as pressing the Forward button twice
window.history.go(2);
```

The location Object

The location object allows you to inspect and change the window's current URL. You can change the current page by setting it to a different string value.

```
window.location = "http://www.google.com";
```

You can also change just part of a URL by assigning new values to any of the following properties. Refer to this example URL:

```
http://www.example.com:8080/dir/file.html?param=value&param2=
➥ value2#comments
```

- **hash** The string after and including the hash: #comments
- **host** The domain and port: www.example.com:8080
- **hostname** Just the domain name: www.example.com
- **href** The entire URL: http://www.example.com:8080/dir/file.html?
  ➥ param=value&param2=value2#comments

- **pathname** The string after the host and before the search, including the leading slash (/): `/dir/file.html`

- **port** The port: `8080`

- **protocol** The string before the host, *not* including the slashes (//): `http:`

- **search** The query string variables, including the leading question mark (?): `?param=value&param2=value2`

Cookies

Cookies are small strings that let you store data across page views and sessions. These are some common uses of cookies:

- Keeping track of whether the user has logged in to your site

- Remembering that a user has visited a page before

- Differentiating between first-time visitors and repeat visitors

Cookies are also sent to the server with every page request. That's how the server knows whether the user is logged in. Because cookies add data to the request and therefore increase the size of the request, cookie data is limited to 4KB.

The `window.document` object has a funny little property called `cookie`. You can use that object to read and set cookie data.

Setting Cookies

To set a cookie, just assign the name and value to `document.cookie` in the following format:

```
document.cookie = "name=value";
```

You can set only one cookie at a time, but assigning another value to document.cookie doesn't overwrite the previous cookies, unless one of them shares the same name. You can continue to assign name/value pairs to document.cookie until you hit the 4KB limit enforced by the browser.

```
// Adding another cookie
document.cookie = "anotherName=anotherValue";
```

You should always pass the value part of the string through encodeURIComponent() to make sure it doesn't contain any illegal characters such as spaces, commas, and semicolons.

```
var cookieValue = "encoded value";
document.cookie = "thirdCookie=" +
➥ encodeURIComponent(cookieValue);
```

You can also set the following optional parameters that affect the visibility, life span, and security of this particular cookie:

- **domain** The domain or subdomain that can read this cookie.

- **expires** The date on which this cookie expires. This must be in GMT format.

- **max-age** The lifetime in seconds before the cookie should expire.

- **path** The URL path to which this cookie is restricted.

- **secure** If set, the browser will send this cookie over HTTPS only for security.

You can set any of these parameters by appending them to the cookie string, separated by semicolons.

```
// This secure cookie will last a year
document.cookie = "name=value;max-age=" + (60*60*24*365) +
➥ ";secure;";
```

note Restricting the visibility of a cookie by setting the domain and path parameters does not make your cookie secure. Never store sensitive information such as usernames and passwords in cookies.

Reading Cookies

Even though document.cookie only lets you set one cookie at a time, you read all the cookie values at once.

```
document.cookie;
"name=value; anotherName=anotherValue; thirdCookie=
➥ encoded%20value"
```

You'll have to use your string manipulation skills to extract a single cookie's value from this string. Regular expressions come in handy here.

```
function getCookie(name) {
    // Get each individual cookie by splitting
    // on semicolons and possible spaces
    var cookies = document.cookie.split(/;\s*/);

    // Make a regular expression to match the name
    // and value in a subpattern
    var pattern = new RegExp("\\b" + name + "=(.*)");

    // Check each cookie until you find a match
    for (var i = 0, l = cookies.length; i < l; i++) {
        var match = cookies[i].match(pattern);
        if (match) {
            return decodeURIComponent(match[1]);
        }
    }
}
getCookie("thirdCookie");
"encoded value"
```

Deleting Cookies

Deleting cookies is simple: Just set the cookie's value to nothing with a max-age of zero.

```
document.cookie = "anotherName=;max-age=0";
```

The navigator Object

The navigator object gives some insight into what browser is running your code. This is sometimes referred to as *browser sniffing*. This is useful for two reasons:

- You can use it to collect data about what browsers visit your sites. This is called *analytics*, and there are many prebuilt solutions for this like Google Analytics.

- You can use it to target code for a particular browser. For instance, if you know that Internet Explorer doesn't support some code, you can test for "Microsoft Internet Explorer" in window.navigator.appName.

Unfortunately, this object isn't as useful as it could be for a couple of reasons:

- There aren't any standards for what type of values navigator properties should have. For instance, window.navigator.appVersion is not just a version number but can include a variety of other information.

- Early JavaScript programmers relied too heavily on this information, so their scripts worked only in certain browsers. When a new browser came out, it would use the navigator properties to pretend to be a different browser. For instance, many sites in the 1990s were built to work best in Netscape. Internet Explorer then copied parts of Netscape's window.navigator.appCodeName in order to trick those sites to run code as if it were Netscape.

Feature Detection vs. Browser Sniffing

In the next few chapters, I'll discuss many properties and methods that some browsers (mainly Internet Explorer) don't support. In your code, you could take one of two approaches to handling these differences:

- You could use the navigator properties to determine whether the browser is Internet Explorer and execute different code.

- You could check to see whether the property or method you want to use exists and execute different code if it doesn't.

The latter method is always the better way to go. If Internet Explorer 10 includes support for the property or method, then your test is no longer applicable. Feature detection—testing for the feature before using it—is the most reliable way to make sure your code continues to work efficiently with future browsers.

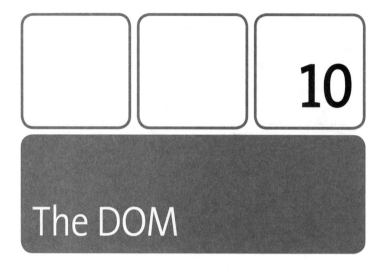

10

The DOM

This chapter could easily be titled something like "Scripting HTML," but the DOM is such an important concept that it deserves marquee status. DOM stands for "Document Object Model," which is a concise way of explaining exactly what it is: the model (or representation) for the objects in an HTML document. More specifically, it is a hierarchy of data types for HTML documents, links, forms, comments, and everything else that can be represented in HTML code.

Like everything else in client-side scripting, the DOM has a muddy history, and resulting implementations across browsers are more complicated for it. Web standards have smoothed out many rough edges, but you still have to account for missing methods and differences in implementations, especially in Internet Explorer. (Chapter 12 will show how to take advantage of code that lets you ignore all these differences.)

Nodes

Nodes are the general data type for objects in the DOM. They have *attributes*, and some nodes can contain other nodes.

There are several node types, which represent more specific data types for HTML elements. Node types are represented by numeric constants, so if you need to determine the type of a node, compare its nodeType property with the values in **Table 10.1**.

Table 10.1 Common Node Types

Type	Constants
Document, the element at the top of the DOM tree	Node.DOCUMENT_NODE === 9
Element, the general type for nodes represented by HTML tags	Node.ELEMENT_NODE === 1
Text, representing simple text in HTML including whitespace	Node.TEXT_NODE === 3
Comment, for `<!-- html comments -->`	Node.COMMENT_NODE === 8
DocumentFragment, the top element for abstract DOM trees	Node.DOCUMENT_FRAGMENT_NODE === 11

Notice that text and comments are also nodes in the DOM, even though it's rare that you'll need to retrieve and manipulate them.

Node Collections

Collections are arraylike objects that hold lists of nodes. Unlike arrays, these lists are "live," meaning that if the DOM changes (nodes are added, removed, or reordered), the collection automatically updates to reflect those changes.

As an example, say you have three paragraphs in your page, like this:

```
<p>one</p>
<p>two</p>
<p>three</p>
```

You can retrieve a collection of those nodes with the
getElementsByTagName() method. Its length property has the value of 3.

```
var paragraphs = document.getElementsByTagName("p");
console.log(paragraphs.length);
3
```

Now, create a new paragraph, and append it to the document body.

```
var newPara = document.createElement("p");
newPara.appendChild(document.createTextNode("four"));
document.body.appendChild(newPara);
```

The collection of paragraphs automatically updates to include the new
paragraph as soon as it is added to the page.

```
console.log(paragraphs.length);
4
```

If you need array methods such as splice() or reverse(), you have to
convert the collection to an array by looping over each item and adding
the items to a real array. However, this new array is not live, so it will not
automatically update to reflect changes to the page.

Node Trees

Nodes are organized in hierarchies, or *trees*. Nodes that contain other nodes
are *parent nodes*. Nodes contained in a parent node are *child nodes*. Text
and comment nodes can be child nodes, but they can't be parent nodes.

An HTML document that looks like the following is represented as a node tree in the DOM:

```
<!DOCTYPE html>
<html>
    <head>
        <title>DOM Example</title
    </head>
    <body>
        <div>
        <h1>Heading</h1>
        </div>
        <p>Click this <a href="#">Link</a> to see more.</p>
    </body>
</html>
```

You could diagram the DOM tree as shown in **Figure 10.1**.

Figure 10.1
A DOM tree diagram.

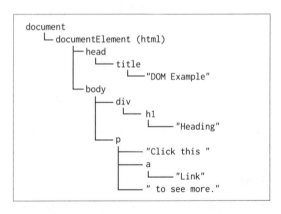

Notice how the <p> element contains three nodes: a text node, an <a> element, and another text node.

This tree diagram is actually missing many more text nodes, because newlines and indentations count as text nodes. The node tree starting at the <div> element should actually look like **Figure 10.2** to include the formatting whitespace.

Figure 10.2
A branch of the DOM tree with whitespace text nodes.

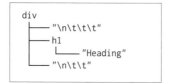

Node Properties

All nodes have three common properties, though some of them are less useful on certain node types.

nodeName

For element nodes, which are represented by <tags> in HTML, the node-Name property is the tag name. In HTML it is always uppercase.

```
document.createElement("a").nodeName;
"A"
document.createElement("fieldset").nodeName;
"FIELDSET"
```

Other node types return a string representation of its type.

```
document.nodeName;
"#document"
document.createTextNode("a text node").nodeName;
"#text"
```

Likewise, the nodeName properties of comment nodes and document fragment nodes return "#comment" and "#document-fragment," respectively.

nodeType

The nodeType property returns a numeric constant, useful for determining the unknown type of a node. Refer to Table 10.1 for various nodeType values.

```
var nodeType = element.firstChild.nodeType;
if (nodeType === 1) {
   console.log("The node is an element");
} else if (nodeType === 3) {
   console.log("The node is a text node");
} else if (nodeType === 8) {
   console.log("The node is a comment");
}
```

nodeValue

The nodeValue property is useful only for text and comment nodes. The property returns null for all other node types.

```
<p>Text node inside of a paragraph <!-- a comment node --></p>

// Retrieve the first item in the collection with [0]
var para = document.getElementsByTagName("p")[0];
para.firstChild.nodeValue; // Text node
"Text node inside of a paragraph "
para.lastChild.nodeValue; // Comment node
" a comment node "
```

Walking the DOM

The simplest way to find DOM nodes is to "walk" the DOM tree. Nodes have several properties that return adjacent nodes in the tree. You can combine these properties to walk from node to node.

Refer to this HTML document for the examples in this section:

```
<!DOCTYPE html>
<html>
    <head>
        <title>Walking the DOM</title>
    </head>
    <body>
        <h1>Heading</h1>
        <p>Paragraph with <a href="#">Link</a></p>
    </body>
</html>
```

Starting with document

The document element is a property of the global window object, so it's the most easily accessed and most used DOM node. It has two important properties that act as starting points in the DOM tree.

```
document.documentElement;
<html>
document.body;
<body>
```

Use the firstChild property to access the <head> element inside the documentElement.

```
document.documentElement.firstChild;
<head>
```

The childNodes property returns a collection, so you can loop over it like an array. In a well-formatted HTML document, you will find many text nodes.

```
var bodyChildNodes = document.body.childNodes;
for (var i = 0, l = bodyChildNodes.length; i < l; i++) {
    console.log(bodyChildNodes[i]);
}
<TextNode textContent="\n ">
<h1>
<TextNode textContent="\n ">
<p>
<TextNode textContent="\n ">
```

The <h1> tag is the second child node of <body>. You can access it by walking from the text node to its next sibling node.

```
document.body.firstChild.nextSibling;
<h1>
```

You can also access it by its index in the childNodes collection.

```
document.body.childNodes[1];
<h1>
```

To retrieve the <p> element, you can continue to walk the tree, skipping over the whitespace between elements.

```
var heading = document.body.childNodes[1];
heading.nextSibling.nextSibling;
<p>
```

The paragraph has two child nodes, including the first useful text node.

```
var paragraph = heading.nextSibling.nextSibling;
paragraph.childNodes;
[<TextNode textContent="Paragraph with ">, a walking.html#]
```

The lastChild property gives you quick access to the <a> node inside the paragraph.

```
paragraph.lastChild;
<a href="#">
```

You can walk back to the <h1> node with previousSibling, again skipping over the whitespace between elements.

```
paragraph.previousSibling.previousSibling;
<h1>
```

You can also walk up the DOM tree to the <body> node with the parentNode property.

```
paragraph.parentNode;
<body>
```

Managing Whitespace

The fact that whitespace appears in the DOM tree makes walking the DOM less useful than it should be. Creating utility methods that skip whitespace text nodes is a common solution.

```
function usefulNextSibling(startingNode) {
    var notWhitespace = /[^\t\n\r\s]/;
    var sibling = startingNode;

    while (sibling = sibling.nextSibling) {
        if (! (sibling.nodeType === 3 &&
        ➥ notWhitespace.test(sibling.nodeValue))) {
            return sibling;                    (continues on next page)
```

```
        }
    }
}
```

```
// Example usage
usefulNextSibling(heading);
<p>
```

The statement while (sibling = sibling.nextSibling) reassigns the value of sibling to its nextSibling until it runs out of elements and the loop stops. The if statement checks whether the sibling is a text node (nodeType === 3) and that it contains characters other than tabs, newlines, and spaces using a regular expression.

Many libraries include useful tree-walking functions to make program-mers' lives easier.

children

Not available in Internet Explorer 6 and 7

Modern browsers provide a new property, children, that returns a collec-tion of child element nodes only, ignoring text and comment nodes. Sadly, it doesn't work in Internet Explorer 6 and 7.

```
document.body.children;
[h1, p]
paragraph.children; // Ignores the nonempty text node
[a walking.html#]
```

Finding Nodes

Walking the DOM is useful for finding elements that are close to one another, but if you need an element deep in the DOM tree, it's much easier to find it with one of these retrieval methods.

getElementById(domId)

The getElementById() method is one of the most common DOM methods. It returns a single element node that has the id attribute of domId.

```
<div id="content">
    <div id="sidebar"></div>
</div>
document.getElementById("content");
<div id="content">
```

getElementsByTagName(name)

The getElementsByTagName() method returns a collection of element nodes with the tag name of name.

All element nodes have these retrieval methods, so you can look for a node inside another node.

```
var content = document.getElementById("content");
content.getElementsByTagName("div");
[ <div class="sidebar"> ]
```

getElementsByClassName(name)

Not available in Internet Explorer

Modern browsers provide a method similar to getElementsByTagName() that retrieves elements by their class attribute. It even finds elements using combinations of classes when separated by a space.

```
<p>Normal paragraph</p>
<p class="special">Special paragraph</p>
<p class="extra special">Special paragraph</p>

document.getElementsByClassName("special");
[ p.special, p.extra ]
document.getElementsByClassName("extra special");
[ p.extra ]
```

You can write a helper function that works similarly to getElementsByClassName() by looping over all the elements in the page and testing for the class name using a regular expression:

```
function getByClass(className, tagName, parentElement) {
   parentElement = parentElement || document;
   tagName = tagName || "*";

   // Use the real method if available
   if (parentElement.getElementsByClassName) {
      return parentElement.getElementsByClassName(className);

   } else {
      var classNameTest = new RegExp("\\b" + className + "\\b");
      var elementsByTag =
      ➥ parentElement.getElementsByTagName(tagName);
      var results = [];
      for (var i = -1, el; el = elementsByTag[++i];) {
         if (classNameTest.test(el.className)) {
            results.push(results);
         }
      }
      return results;
```

```
    }
}
```

It would be too expensive to loop over every element in the page when you use this helper function, so you can specific a tag name or a parent element to search through a smaller collection of elements. This example limits its search to <p> elements inside an element with the ID of "parentId":

```
var parent = document.getElementById("parentId");
getByClass("special", "p", parent);
```

querySelector(selector)

Not available in Internet Explorer 6 or 7

The querySelector() method is a new method that uses the browser's CSS selector engine to find elements in a page. It returns the *first* element that matches selector. You can use any CSS selector that the browser supports.

For simple selectors, you're better off using one of the getElement* methods because they are always faster.

```
document.querySelector("#domId"); // Akin to getElementById()
document.querySelector(".name");
➥ // getElementsByClassName()
document.querySelector("div"); // getElementsByTagName()
```

The real power of querySelector() is the ability to search the document with complex, chained selectors.

```
document.querySelector("#parent + .adjacent >
➥ .directDescendent a:last-child");
```

querySelectorAll(selector)

Not available in Internet Explorer 6 or 7

The querySelectorAll() method works the same as querySelector() except that it returns all elements that match selector. Unlike getElementsByTagName(), querySelectorAll() returns a static list that doesn't automatically update when the DOM changes.

Creating Nodes

The DOM provides a few methods to create new nodes. In addition, Microsoft created a nonstandard way of creating nodes that had enough benefits to be adopted by modern browsers.

Using DOM Methods

The DOM methods are great for when you want to create one node at a time.

createElement(tagName)

Creating element nodes is as simple as passing the desired tag name to document.createElement(). Unlike many DOM methods, createElement() is available only on the document object.

```
document.createElement("div");
<div>
document.createElement("a");
<a>
document.createElement("body");
<body>
```

Creating HTML5 Elements

HTML5 introduces several new elements for richer semantics and better document structure, such as <article>, <aside>, and <nav>. By default, Internet Explorer handles these new elements so poorly that they become unusable. Fortunately, you can pass any tag name to createElement(). Creating a single copy of a new element causes Internet Explorer to treat it as if it were a <div>.

```
document.createElement("nav");
```

There are a few "HTML5 shim" scripts available online that add support for all of the new HTML5 elements.

createTextNode(nodeValue)

You can use the createTextNode() method to add text inside an element node.

```
<p id="myPara"></p>
```

```
var textNode = document.createTextNode("Inserted Text");
document.getElementById("myPara").appendChild(textNode);
<TextNode textContent="Inserted Text">
```

The paragraph element now looks like this:

```
<p id="myPara">Inserted Text</p>
```

cloneNode(deep)

You can create a copy of a node with cloneNode(). The deep argument is required. If deep is true, cloneNode() copies the entire tree of the node, including all element and text nodes. If it is `false`, it copies only the node in question.

```
<p id="myPara">Click <a href="#">here</a>.</p>

var myPara = document.getElementById("myPara");
var deepClone = myPara.cloneNode(true);
var shallowClone = myPara.cloneNode(false);
deepClone.childNodes.length;
3
shallowClone.childNodes.length;
0
```

Using innerHTML

Microsoft created the `innerHTML` property on element nodes as a quick-and-dirty way of setting the HTML contents of an element. Simply assign the property to a string with HTML tags.

```
var myPara = document.getElementById("myPara");
myPara.innerHTML = 'Click <a href="#">here</a>.';
```

Regardless of the former contents of `myPara`, it now looks like the following because `innerHTML` completely overwrites the element's content:

```
<p id="myPara">Click <a href="#">here</a>.</p>
```

You can now retrieve the newly created `<a>` tag like so:

```
var newLink = myPara.getElementsByTagName("a")[0];
```

The benefit of this technique is that you can make massive changes to the DOM with only a single line of code. Achieving the same result with `createElement()` and `createTextNode()` requires many more method calls and lines of code.

A potential downside is that it treats HTML as strings in JavaScript source code. This can quickly become unwieldy, because you have to balance single quotes and double quotes in long strings. HTML code in JavaScript makes your code harder to read and maintain.

Using Document Fragments

Every time you change the DOM, the browser updates the page to reflect those changes. This is called a *repaint*. Repainting large or complex pages can cause the browser to halt or stutter as it recalculates the display of each DOM node.

If you need to make many changes to the DOM all at once, you can make those changes to a document fragment node and avoid repaints after each change. Once you finish the changes, you can pull the results from the fragment to update the document.

```
var fragment = document.createDocumentFragment();

// Create 100 new paragraphs with createElement()
for (var i = 0; i < 100; i++) {
    var para = document.createElement("p");
    para.appendChild(document.createTextNode("Paragraph " + i));
    fragment.appendChild(para);
}

// Add all of them to the document at once
document.body.appendChild(fragment);
```

Adding, Removing, and Reordering Nodes

These methods actually work the same across browsers, so they're very useful to know.

appendChild(node)

The appendChild() method adds node as the last child node.

```
document.body.appendChild(document.createTextNode(
➥ "Appended Text"));
```

insertBefore(node, reference)

The insertBefore() methods inserts node directly before reference.

```
<p id="p1">First Paragraph</p>
<p id="p3">Third Paragraph</p>

var thirdPara = document.getElementById("p3");
var secondPara = document.createElement("p");
secondPara.appendChild(document.createTextNode(
➥ "Second Paragraph"));
thirdPara.parentNode.insertBefore(secondPara, thirdPara);
```

removeChild(childNode)

The removeChild() method removes and returns childNode from the DOM. Note that you don't have to call removeChild() before appendChild() or insertBefore() if you're manipulating a node that's already part of the document. Nodes are automatically removed before they are inserted into a new location in the DOM tree.

Utility Functions

The DOM doesn't provide prependChild() or insertAfter(), but these functions are relatively simple to write yourself.

```
function prependChild(parent, node) {
   // If the parent has children, insert the node
   // before the parent's firstChild
   if (parent.firstChild) {
      parent.insertBefore(node, parent.firstChild);

   // If the parent is empty, just append the node
   } else {
      parent.appendChild(node);
   }
   return node;
}

// Example usage
prependChild(parent, newChildNode);

function insertAfter(node, reference) {
   // If the reference node has a nextSibling, insert
   // the node before that
   if (reference.nextSibling) {
      reference.parentNode.insertBefore(node,
      ➥ reference.nextSibling);

   // If the reference node is the last child, just
   // append the node to the parent
   } else {
      reference.parentNode.appendChild(node);
   }
   return node;
}

// Example usage
insertAfter(newNode, referenceNode);
```

Prototypes of DOM Nodes

DOM nodes aren't true JavaScript objects but instead are *interfaces* to the elements in the HTML document. The actual implementation of these interfaces is complicated and varies across browsers, but the end result is that you can't reliably manipulate the prototypes of their data types. For example, you can't add an `insertAfter()` method to all DOM elements like I added `trim()` to all strings in Chapter 6.

Most JavaScript libraries instead create wrapper objects for DOM nodes in order to add methods and code in an object-oriented style. Here is a simple example so that the concept is more familiar once you start using libraries:

```
var Wrapper = function(node) {
   this.node = node;
};

Wrapper.prototype = {
   // Implement built-in methods
   appendChild : function(child) {
      return this.node.appendChild(child);
   },

   // Implement custom methods
   prependChild : function(child) {
      if (this.node.firstChild) {
         return this.node.insertBefore(child,
         ➥ this.node.firstChild);
      } else {
         return this.node.appendChild(child);
      }
```

(continues on next page)

Prototypes of DOM Nodes (continued)

```
    }
};

var wrappedNode = new Wrapper(document.
getElementById("domId"));
wrappedNode.appendChild(newNode);
wrappedNode.prependChild(anotherNode);
```

Inspecting and Changing Elements

Finding and creating DOM elements are important steps, but JavaScript
programmers spend far more time using and changing the various properties and attributes of DOM elements.

Attributes

HTML elements, such as <a> and <input>, have a bunch of attributes,
such as href and type, that determine their appearance and functionality in a Web page. In JavaScript, they are available as simple properties
that you can read and assign new values with the dot (.) or bracket ([])
operators.

```
<a href="http://www.google.com">Search Engine</a>
<input type="text" name="name" id="name" value="" />

var link = document.getElementsByTagName("a")[0];
link.href;
```
```
"http://www.google.com"
```
(continues on next page)

```
link.href = "http://www.bing.com";
"http://www.bing.com"

var nameInput = document.getElementById("name");
nameInput.type;
"text"
nameInput["value"] = "Lenny";
"Lenny"
```

note Internet Explorer throws an error if you try to change the type attribute of an input. Nearly all HTML attributes are mutable, but this is an exception because of a browser bug.

Two common attribute names, class and for, conflict with reserved words in JavaScript, so you must refer to them as className and htmlFor.

```
link.className = "special";
```

Calculated Attribute Values

When you access an element's attribute with a property, the value may not exactly match the HTML source code. Attribute properties are calculated values, which are usually more useful, fortunately.

Relative link href values often leave out the "http://" and the domain, but the href property always returns a fully qualified URL.

```
<a href="a/relative/page.html">Link</a>
link.href;
"http://www.example.com/a/relative/page.html"
```

Also, attributes such as checked and selected for <input> elements don't really have a value. Their presence in the HTML code indicates a true value.

```
<input type="radio" id="radio1" checked="checked" />
<input type="radio" id="radio2" />

var radio1 = document.getElementById("radio1");
var radio2 = document.getElementById("radio2");
radio1.checked;
true
radio2.checked;
false
radio2.checked = true; // radio2 is now checked
```

The DOM provides a few methods for handling attributes, but I much prefer the object property syntax described earlier because it's more succinct. The getAttribute() method is sometimes useful, however, because it doesn't return a calculated value. (Link href attributes require special treatment in Internet Explorer to get the uncalculated value.)

```
<a href="relative.html" id="special">Special Link</a>

var link = document.getElementById("special");
link.getAttribute("id");
"special"
link.hasAttribute("class");
false
link.setAttribute("class", "normal");
link.removeAttribute("id");

// For most browsers
link.getAttribute("href");
"relative.html"
// For Internet Explorer (notice the 2)
link.getAttribute("href", 2);
"relative.html"
```

You should always use attributes with explicit values such as `<input checked="checked" />` (instead of `<input checked />`), especially if you're using the `getAttribute()` method.

Special Properties

DOM elements have a few special read-only properties to determine element dimensions and positions. They are fairly reliable across all browsers, but there are some quirks in special situations. Generally speaking, I prefer to use library functions such as jQuery's `width()`, `height()`, and `offset()` methods to make life easier.

Size is relatively straightforward: The `offsetWidth` and `offsetHeight` properties return pixel values representing the width and height of an element, respectively.

The `offsetLeft` and `offsetTop` properties aren't quite as simple, because elements are positioned relative to their *offset parent*, which is available on the `offsetParent` property.

When you want to change the position of an element with CSS, you change its `position` property to "absolute" or "relative" and set the position with `top` or `left`.

```css
#positioned {
    position: absolute;
    left: 100px;
    top: 50px;
}
```

If the element exists inside another positioned element, the values for `top` and `left` start counting from the top-left corner of that parent element.

```
#offsetParent {
    position: relative;
}

<div id="offsetParent">
    <div id="positioned"></div>
</div>
```

If the #offsetParent element exists at left: 200px, top: 200px, then the #positioned element really sits at left: 300px, top: 250px (**Figure 10.3**). But its offsetLeft and offsetTop properties just return 100 and 50, respectively.

Figure 10.3
How offsetLeft *and* offsetTop *work.*

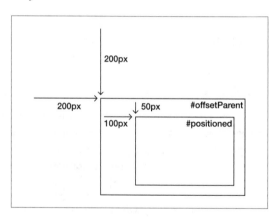

These helper functions are useful for finding the position of an element in the document by looping through every offsetParent.

```
function getLeft(element) {
    var left = element.offsetLeft;
    while (element = element.offsetParent) {
        left += element.offsetLeft;               (continues on next page)
```

```
    }
    return left;
}

function getTop(element) {
    var top = element.offsetTop;
    while (element = element.offsetParent) {
        top += element.offsetTop;
    }
    return top;
}
```

Element Styles

Changing the appearance of an element is probably the most common task in JavaScript programming. In fact, I would say that, at a basic level, most of the user interface components I build do little more than change the styles of elements in various ways.

JavaScript and CSS are very powerful, but they're such different technologies that it takes a while to understand how to use them together. Browser APIs and incompatibilities don't make it any easier, either. After events, the second most important reason why I use JavaScript libraries is reading and writing element styles.

You can do plenty of things with plain JavaScript, classes, and the style property, though.

The class Attribute

The easiest and often most effective way to change an element's appearance is to change the CSS that affects it by changing its class. If you want to hide an element, you can use this:

```
/* In your CSS code */
.hide {
    display: none
}
```

```
// In JavaScript
element.className = "hide";
```

To revert the element to its original state, just remove the "hide" class. The tasks of adding, removing, and toggling classes are so common that nearly every JavaScript library includes functions to facilitate them.

It's an effective best practice to put all your appearance-related code in the CSS and just use class names in JavaScript. Imagine your site highlights special text by changing the color to red. You could litter your JavaScript with code like this:

```
text.style.color = "red";
```

But if your design changes and you want to highlight text in blue, you have to change every reference to "red" in your JavaScript files. A better solution would be to use a "highlight" class to keep all your color references in CSS.

```
/* In your CSS */
.highlight {
    color: blue;
}
```

```
// Using a JavaScript function provided by a library
addClass(text, "highlight");
```

The style Attribute

The style attribute is special in JavaScript. In HTML, it allows you to write inline CSS for a specific element.

```
<p style="font-family: monospace; background-color: #fcc;
➥ margin-bottom: 10px">Text</p>
```

In JavaScript, an element's style property is a special object with properties for every CSS property.

```
p.style.fontFamily = "monospace";
p.style.backgroundColor = "#fcc";
p.style.marginBottom = "10px";
```

Take note of two really important details about that example:

- CSS properties with multiple words are referenced in camelCase in JavaScript.

- Values for style properties are always strings. Numbers still need units like "px" or "em."

You can assign values freely to style properties. If the browser's CSS engine doesn't understand a value, it will be ignored.

There are nearly limitless uses for style properties, but they require a solid understanding of CSS to be used effectively.

Reading values from the style property can be confusing at first. Values come from the actual style attribute in the HTML, not from CSS.

```
#styled {
    width: 100px;
}

<div id="styled" style="height: 100px"></div>
```

```
var div = document.getElementById("styled");
div.style.height;
"100px"
div.style.width;
""
```

Style properties aren't very useful for inspecting the appearance of an element, unless you've set the styles in HTML or with JavaScript. That's where computed styles come in.

Computed Styles

The DOM provides an API for retrieving the computed value of an element's style. Unfortunately, not only is it very awkward to use, but Internet Explorer has its own incompatible version. I usually leave this work to a JavaScript library, but here is how it basically works if you're interested:

```
// The standard API
document.defaultView.getComputedStyle(element,
➡ null).getPropertyValue("width");

// The Microsoft API
element.currentStyle("width");
```

The standard API is long and ugly, but it at least works how you want it. The Microsoft API is actually pretty nice, except that it doesn't always return useful values. Width, height, position, and font size values are returned literally from the CSS, so sometimes they are percentages, in ems, or even just "auto." JavaScript libraries use a number of tricks to turn these relative values into absolute pixels, which are far more useful in JavaScript.

11

Events

Events are hugely important to client-side programming. Without them, you couldn't add interactivity to web pages beyond clicking links and submitting forms.

Using events is a matter of executing a function in response to an action or input. These functions are known as event *listeners* or event *handlers*. I prefer *handler* even though some method names use *listener*. (Would a function handle an event or listen for an event? The former makes more sense to me.)

You can add event handlers to page elements in two ways, and Internet Explorer throws a wrench into the works by providing a completely different event API from every other modern browser. Handling events properly across all browsers can be pretty tricky, but fortunately JavaScript libraries make it much easier by abstracting away all the messy details. Cross-browser event handling is the biggest reason why I almost always use a library when programming JavaScript.

This chapter introduces event handling in pure JavaScript, followed by examples for the different event types. That way, you can have a sense of what's going on under the hood when you use JavaScript library event functions in the examples later in the book.

Event Attributes

The simplest way to add an event handler is to assign a function to an event attribute of a DOM element. Event attributes have names like onclick, onkeypress, and onload.

```
var link = document.getElementsByTagName("a")[0];
function clickHandler() {
    alert(this.href);
    return false;
}
link.onclick = clickHandler;
```

Assuming there is a link in your HTML document, clicking it shows an alert dialog box with the href value of the link. The browser won't follow the link because its default behavior is prevented.

This style of event handling works the same across all browsers. For simple tasks, it's a great way to start working with events.

Event Attributes in HTML

I'm referring to this style of event handling as *event attributes* and
not *properties* because you can use them as HTML attributes.

```
<a href="http://www.google.com" onclick="alert(this.href);
➥ return false; ">Click Here</a>
```

I won't show any more examples of this style of code because it's
always best to avoid mixing your HTML and JavaScript.

Return Values

Handlers on event attributes can prevent the default behavior of an
event by returning false. For click events on links, this prevents the
browser from following the link and loading a new page. For submit
events on forms, this prevents the form from submitting and loading a
new page.

```
var form = document.getElementsByTagName("form")[0];
function preventSubmit() {
    return false;
}
form.onsubmit = preventSubmit;
```

Event Attribute Method Context

The browser executes event attribute handlers in the context of the
elements to which they were bound. This means you can access the
element with the this keyword.

```
function whatDidIClickOn() {
    console.log("You clicked on ", this);
    return false;
}
var links = document.getElementsByTagName("a");
for (var i = -1, link; link = links[++i];) {
    link.onclick = whatDidIClickOn;
}
You clicked on <a href="http://www.google.com">
```

Multiple Event Handlers

One problem with event attributes is that you can assign only one function to them at a time. You may need an event to execute two different functions. This is common for the onload event. Many scripts add event handlers to the window object's onload event so that they wait until the page finishes loading before running any code. Fortunately, this isn't too hard to overcome.

```
<!DOCTYPE html>
<html>
    <head>
        <title>Multiple Load Handlers</title>
    </head>
    <body>
        <script type="text/javascript">
            function addOnloadHandler(newHandler) {
                var previousHandler = window.onload;
                window.onload = function() {
                    if (typeof previousHandler === "function") {
                        previousHandler.call(this);
                    }
```

```
                newHandler.call(this);
        };
    }
    addOnloadHandler(function() {
        alert("first handler");
    });
    addOnloadHandler(function() {
        alert("second handler");
    });
    </script>
  </body>
</html>
```

The addOnloadHandler() function saves a reference to the current value of window.onload before assigning it a new value. This lets you call both the original event handler and the new event handler when the load event occurs.

The actual event handler ends up being an anonymous function that retains access to both the previousHandler and newHandler variables. It checks to see whether the previousHandler is a function before calling it. Using call() allows you to execute the event handlers in the proper context so that this refers to window.

Event Methods

The DOM provides a more modern and flexible API for handling events. The core methods are commonly referred to as the DOM Level 2 Event API. (Using event attributes, as described earlier, is sometimes referred to as the DOM Level 0 API.) None of these methods work in Internet Explorer.

addEventListener(eventType, handler, capture)

The addEventListener() method explains its purpose right in the name.
The eventType argument is a string for the type, like "submit," "mouseover,"
or "keypress." The handler is a function. And capture is a required Boolean
value that I'll describe in a moment. It will be false in most cases.

```
<p id="para">Click here</p>

var para = document.getElementById("para");
para.addEventListener("click", eventHandler, false);
para.addEventListener("click", otherEventHandler, false);

function eventHandler(event) {
    alert("You clicked a " + this.nodeName);
}
function otherEventHandler(event) {
    alert("This was a " + event.type + " event");
}
```

Clicking the paragraph element should result in two alert dialogs that
say, "You clicked a P" and "This was a click event."

You *cannot* be sure which event handler will execute first. It's entirely up
to the browser to decide the order.

As you can see, it's much easier to attach multiple events to elements with
this style of adding event handlers. Generally speaking, it's considered the
better and more modern approach to events compared to event attributes.

removeEventListener(eventType, handler, capture)

The removeEventListener() method is also self-explanatory. All arguments work exactly as they do in addEventListener(). To remove
a particular event handler, pass in the same arguments you used in
addEventListener().

```
<h1 id="header">Click this multiple times</h1>

var header = document.getElementById("header");
header.addEventListener("click", selfRemovingEvent, false);

function selfRemovingEvent(event) {
    alert("Listening for the event and removing myself");
    this.removeEventListener(event.type, selfRemovingEvent,
    ➥false);
}
```

This event handler removes itself after being called, so you will see the alert dialog only once. You have to pass the original function to removeEventListener(), so you can't use anonymous functions in this case.

The Internet Explorer API

Internet Explorer's event API is different and inconvenient enough that I never use it. Not only does it work differently than the standard API, but it also has problems with memory leaks. If an event handler references another DOM element, sometimes that element becomes trapped in memory and eventually bogs down the browser.

You can write a function that uses the standard API or the Internet Explorer API depending on what's available, but JavaScript libraries already handle that and do it better. You can look forward to handling cross-browser events with APIs like this:

```
link.bind("click", function(event) {
    alert("Don't go to " + this.href);
    event.preventDefault();
});
```

The Event Object

Using the standard API, event handlers receive an Event object as an argument. This object provides information about the event as well as methods for controlling the outcome and life cycle of the event.

Properties

Different types of events have different properties, which you'll learn about later in the chapter. Here are a few properties common to all standard Event objects:

- **type** The type of the event, like "click," "load," or "keypress."

- **target** The element that originally dispatched the event. This may not be the same as the element to which the event handler is attached.

- **currentTarget** The element to which you attached the event handler. In most cases, it is synonymous with the `this` keyword. If you change the context of the event handler with `call()` or `apply()`, you can still access the element with `currentTarget`.

- **eventPhase** A number that indicates whether the event is currently capturing (1), bubbling (3), or at the target element (2). Find out more information in the "Event Bubbling and Capturing" section later in this chapter.

- **timeStamp** A number in seconds that represents the time at which the event occurred.

Methods

These methods give you control over the how long the event lives and what its final outcome is.

- **preventDefault()** Prevents the default behavior from occurring. Default behaviors include following links and submitting forms.

```
<a id="link" href="http://www.google.com">Don't go to
↪ Google</a>

var link = document.getElementById("link");
link.addEventListener("click", dontFollowLink, false);

function dontFollowLink(event) {
 alert("Not going to " + this.href);
 event.preventDefault();
}
```

- **stopPropagation()** Stops the event from continuing to propagate through the DOM tree. Find out more information in the "Event Bubbling and Capturing" section.

Event Objects in Internet Explorer

In Internet Explorer, the Event object isn't available as an argument of the handler. Instead, it's a property of window. To write cross-browser DOM Level 0 code, look for the Event object in both places.

```
function handler(event) {
    event = event || window.event;
}
```

Event Bubbling and Capturing

The life cycle of an Event object is more complicated than you may initially expect. Events go through three phases and travel up and down the DOM tree when they fire. Most of the time this doesn't come into play, but it's still an important concept to understand.

Bubbling

When an event occurs on an element, it triggers on all the parent nodes of that element. You can test this for yourself. Make an HTML document with this body:

```
<body>
    <div>
        <p>
            <a href="http://www.google.com">Click</a>
        </p>
    </div>
</body>
```

Add some padding to the elements too so you can click a parent element without clicking the child:

```
body, div, p {
    padding: 10px;
}
```

Then add a script block that adds an event listener to each element and the document. (Remember, this code won't work in IE.)

```
var div = document.getElementsByTagName("div")[0];
var p = document.getElementsByTagName("p")[0];
var a = document.getElementsByTagName("a")[0];

document.addEventListener("click", whatNode, false);
document.body.addEventListener("click", whatNode, false);
div.addEventListener("click", whatNode, false);
p.addEventListener("click", whatNode, false);
a.addEventListener("click", whatNode, false);
```

```
function whatNode(event) {
    console.log(this.nodeName);
    event.preventDefault();
}
```

When you click the link, the console shows this:

```
A
P
DIV
BODY
#document
```

If you just click the <div> element, the event handlers for the <a> and <p> elements won't execute:

```
DIV
BODY
#document
```

The Event object *bubbles* from the target element through each element in the DOM tree all the way up to the document. If you add an event handler to an element, any child element can cause that handler to execute.

This is important enough to repeat: Events firing on the children of an element cause the element's event handlers to execute. Because the document object is an ancestor of all elements in the page, its event handlers always execute regardless of where the event originated.

Capturing

The bubbling phase is actually the last phase of an Event object's life cycle. All events originate on the document and travel down the DOM tree to the target element. This is called the *capture* phase.

To add an event handler to the capture phase of an event, change the third argument in addEventListener() to true. Add these lines to the HTML document you created to test bubbling:

```
document.addEventListener("click", whatNode, true);
document.body.addEventListener("click", whatNode, true);
div.addEventListener("click", whatNode, true);
p.addEventListener("click", whatNode, true);
a.addEventListener("click", whatNode, true);
```

Also, change the whatNode() function to this:

```
function whatNode(event) {
    console.log(this.nodeName, "phase: " + event.eventPhase);
    event.preventDefault();
}
```

Now when you click the link, the console shows this:

```
#document phase: 1
BODY phase: 1
DIV phase: 1
P phase: 1
A phase: 2
A phase: 2
P phase: 3
DIV phase: 3
BODY phase: 3
#document phase: 3
```

As the event travels from the document to the target element, it's in the capture phase, represented by the 1. At the target element, the event is in the second "at target" phase. The last phase is the bubbling phase, which you've seen before.

Stop Propagation

You can stop an element from continuing to capture or bubble by calling stopPropagation() on the Event object. Change the whatNode() function to demonstrate this.

```
function whatNode(event) {
    if (this.nodeName === "DIV") {
        event.stopPropagation();
    }
    console.log(this.nodeName, "phase: " + event.eventPhase);
    event.preventDefault();
}
```

Clicking the link now results in this:

```
#document phase: 1
BODY phase: 1
DIV phase: 1
```

With this event handler, the event stops propagating down the DOM tree once it reaches the <div> element during the capture phase.

Event Delegation

Understanding bubbling and capturing is mostly important for knowing how child elements affect the event handlers of their parents. But it also has a practical use with a technique called *event delegation*.

Say you have a page with 100 links and want to do something special when the user clicks any of them. You could loop through all the links and attach event handlers to each of them.

```
var allLinks = document.getElementsByTagName("a");
var i = allLinks.length;                          (continues on next page)
```

```
while (i--) {
    allLinks[i].addEventListener("click", somethingSpecial,
    ➥ false);
}

function somethingSpecial(event) {
    alert(this.href);
    event.preventDefault();
}
```

But what if you later add links to the page, maybe with an Ajax call?
You'll have to add the event handler to that link too, probably by repeat-
ing the line of code for addEventListener().

A more elegant solution involves adding a single event handler to the
document and having it act based on the target element of the event.

```
// Add one event handler to the capture phase
document.addEventListener("click", delegatedSomethingSpecial,
➥ true);

function delegatedSomethingSpecial(event) {
    if (event.target.nodeName === "A") {
        alert(event.target.href);
        event.preventDefault();
    }
}
```

This new event handler doesn't do anything unless the element that
originated the event is a link. You can add dozens more links to the page,
and this handler will work for all of them. It's also slightly faster because
you're using the capture phase of the event. That way, the event doesn't
travel through all phases of the event life cycle before executing.

Event Examples

Adding/removing event handlers is the same regardless of the type of event. Handling events, however, differs depending on the event type. Here are examples of common event types.

Browser Events

These events are triggered by the browser, not by the user. They're very important but not entirely all that interesting.

load

Most scripts need to wait until the page finishes loading before executing. The simplest way to do this is by adding an event handler on the window object. You usually want to add the event handler as soon as possible, maybe even before any third-party code loads. In that case, use the onload event attribute, but make sure not to override any event handlers already added to the page. See the addOnloadHandler() function discussed earlier in the chapter for an example.

You can also add load event handlers to <img> elements. Unfortunately, you can't rely on them because Internet Explorer may not fire the event if the image is cached on the user's computer.

unload

The unload event fires right before the browser unloads the page, usually to travel to another page. If your page is a complex Web application like Google Docs, you may want to save recent changes to the server with Ajax before the user loads a new page.

beforeunload

The beforeunload event is a special event that is also useful for complex Web applications. It allows you to warn the user that they're about to leave the page. The event handler can return a message for a confirmation dialog to inform the user of the consequences of leaving the page.

```
window.onbeforeunload = function() {
    return "Leaving the page will lose all your work!";
};
```

The entire dialog will say, "Are you sure you want to navigate away from this page? Leaving the page will lose all your work! Press OK to continue, or Cancel to stay on the current page."

resize

The resize event is useful for redrawing a complex layout based on the size of the window.

```
window.onresize = function() {
    var div = document.getElementById("centeredBox");
    var windowHeight = window.innerHeight ||
    ➥ document.documentElement.clientHeight;
    div.style.top = windowHeight / 2 - div.offsetHeight / 2
    ➥ + "px";
};
window.onload = function() {
    window.onresize();
};
```

This example centers a <div> element vertically in the browser, which isn't possible with just CSS. It calls the onresize() method as soon as possible to force the browser to position the <div> when the page loads.

DOMContentLoaded

The DOMContentLoaded event is relatively new and poorly supported across browsers, especially Internet Explorer and nearly all browsers released before 2009. But it's important enough that nearly all JavaScript libraries emulate it as best as possible.

The load event waits until all the resources in the page finish loading before firing. Images, style sheets, and scripts can delay the load event. The DOMContentLoaded event fires as soon as all the DOM elements in the page are available. This lets you manipulate elements in the page as soon as possible.

```
document.addEventListener("DOMContentLoaded", function() {
    // All DOM elements are now available, but the browser
    // might still be loading images and other files
}, false);
```

If you don't include your <script> tags at the bottom of the HTML markup, you'll need to use the DOMContentLoaded event to make sure your DOM elements exist before using them in JavaScript.

Mouse Events

JavaScript lets you take advantage of the versatility of the mouse in many ways. Mouse events provide some useful information about the event, including where it took place and whether the user was holding down any keys during the event.

- **clientX**, **clientY** The mouse position compared to the top-left corner of the viewport (the window).

- **pageX**, **pageY** The mouse position compared to the top-left corner of the page, which may be scrolled out of view.

- **screenX**, **screenY** The mouse position compared to the top-left corner of the computer screen.

- **offsetX**, **offsetY** The mouse position compared to the top-left corner of the element on which the event occurred.

- **altKey**, **ctrlKey**, **metaKey**, **shiftKey** Evaluates to true if, respectively, the Alt, Ctrl, meta, or Shift key is down during the event. The meta key is the Cmd key on Mac OS, so Internet Explorer doesn't support it (being Windows-only).

- **button** Indicates the button used, so it works only on events that involve mouse buttons. The left button is 0, the middle button is 1, and the right button is 2.

- **detail** For mouse button events, the number of times the user clicked the mouse button, if the clicks occur quickly enough together. For mouse wheel events, the distance the wheel has spun.

- **relatedTarget** For mouseover events, the elements that the mouse just left. For mouseout events, the element that the mouse just entered.

click

The click event is the most important because it's not strictly a mouse event (which is why it doesn't have *mouse* in the name like most other events shown next). The keyboard can also trigger click events by hitting Enter/Return on a focused element. This event fires *after* mouse-down and mouseup.

```
<a href="#" id="myLink">Click or hit enter on this element</a>

var link = document.getElementById("myLink");
link.onclick = function(event) {
    alert("clicked!");
};
```

Try tabbing to the link and hitting Enter/Return to see if you can fire the `click` event with the keyboard. It's a lot easier to use `click` than attaching events on both `mouseup` and `keyup`.

mousedown, mouseup

The `mousedown` event is the first event to fire when the user clicks a mouse button.

The `mouseup` event fires when the user releases the mouse button, right before the `click` event fires.

dblclick

The `dblclick` method fires after any other mouse button events. It's very difficult to distinguish between single clicks and double clicks. The `detail` property, which isn't available in older versions of Internet Explorer, gives you a count of the number of clicks.

```
<a href="#" id="myLink">Click this twice</a>

var link = document.getElementById("myLink");
link.onclick = function(event) {
    // Prevent the default behavior or you won't have
    // time to click again and fire the dblclick event
    return false;
};
link.ondblclick = function(event) {
    alert("double clicked!");
};
```

mouseover, mouseout

When the mouse enters an element, the mouseover event fires. When the
mouse leaves, the mouseout event fires. These events are actually tricky to
use because of event bubbling. Create an HTML document with this CSS
and markup:

```
div {
    width: 50px;
    height: 50px;
}

#parent {
    padding: 20px;
    background: #999;
}

#child {
    background: #fff;
}

<div id="parent">
    <div id="child">
    </div>
</div>
```

Now add a `<script>` block that adds mouseover and mouseout event
handlers to the parent element:

```
var parent = document.getElementById("parent");
parent.onmouseover = function(event) {
    console.log("mouseover event occurred");
};
```

```
parent.onmouseout = function(event) {
    console.log("mouseout event occurred");
};
```

When the mouse enters the gray parent <div>, the mouseover event
fires. But if the mouse continues into the white child <div>, the mouseout
and mouseover events fire again. If you only wanted to know when the
mouse enters and leaves the parent <div>, these extra events can be
problematic.

mouseenter, mouseleave

Only available in Internet Explorer

Internet Explorer provides two events that fix the mouseover/mouseout
problem described earlier. The mouseenter and mouseleave events are
the same as mouseover and mouseout, respectively, except that they don't
bubble. For browsers that don't support these events, you can emulate
them with event.relatedTarget.

```
parent.onmouseover = function(event) {
    var related = event.relatedTarget;

    while (related && related !== this) {
        related = related.parentNode;
    }

    if (related !== this) {
        console.log("mouseenter (not mouseover) event occurred");
    }
};
parent.onmouseout = function(event) {
    var related = event.relatedTarget;          (continues on next page)
```

```
    while (related && related !== this) {
        related = related.parentNode;
    }

    if (related !== this) {
        console.log("mouseleave (not mouseout) event occurred");
    }
};
```

The trick behind these event handlers is testing to see whether the
relatedEvent is a child of the parent <div>. Iterating up the DOM
tree with while and parentNode is the quickest way to test this. Some
JavaScript libraries have built-in support for mouseenter and mouseleave.

Keyboard Events

Keyboard events have two properties related to which key the user
pressed: keyCode and charCode. Unfortunately, these properties work
differently depending on the browser and operating system. The user's
language also makes a difference, since different languages use different
keyboard layouts. Generally speaking, keyCode is a number representing a
particular key on the keyboard, and charCode is the character code of the
key pressed. It's best to let a JavaScript library smooth out the differences.

keydown

The keydown event occurs when the user presses a key. Nearly any key
on the keyboard can fire this event, and it always fires before keypress.

keypress

The keypress event occurs only when the user presses a key that
normally prints a character. Keys like Enter/Return and Shift do not fire
this event. The event also repeats while the user holds the key down.

keyup

The keyup event occurs when the user releases the key as the last keyboard event after keydown and keypress.

To demonstrate how confusing the key events can be, here's an example script you can run on any browser:

```
<input type="text" name="textInput" value="" id="textInput" />

var input = document.getElementById("textInput");

function keyReport(event) {
   event = event || window.event;

   var keyCode = event.keyCode;
   var keyCharacter = String.fromCharCode(keyCode);

   var charCode = event.charCode;
   var charCharacter = String.fromCharCode(charCode);

   var report = [
      "Event: " + event.type,
      "Key: " + keyCode + ", " + keyCharacter,
      "Char: " + charCode + ", " + charCharacter
   ].join("\n");

   alert(report);
}

input.onkeydown = keyReport;
input.onkeypress = keyReport;
```

The browser will show you two alert dialogs when you press any key while typing in the text input. Here's what Firefox shows when you press the A key:

Event: keydown
Key: 65, A
Char: 0,

Event: keypress
Key: 0,
Char: 97, a

In this case, the keyCode attribute works only for the keydown and keyup events. The value represents the key pressed, not the letter pressed, so it gives you an uppercase A.

Furthermore, the charCode attribute works only for the keypress event. The value represents the letter pressed, so it gives you a lowercase *a*.

By contrast, the same action in Internet Explorer 8 results in these alert messages:

Event: keydown
Key: 65, A
Char: undefined,

Event: keydown
Key: 97, a
Char: undefined,

Form Element Events

All of the previous events work on form elements such as <input> and <select>, but forms also have a few special events.

change

The change event occurs after the user changes the value of an editable element. It usually occurs after any mouse or keyboard events.

```
<select name="select" id="mySelect">
   <option value="4">Option 1</option>
   <option value="8">Option 2</option>
   <option value="15">Option 3</option>
</select>

var select = document.getElementById("mySelect");
select.onchange = function(event) {
   var newValue = this.options[this.selectedIndex].value;
   alert("New value is " + newValue);
};
```

submit

The submit event applies only to <form> elements. It occurs when the user submits a form. You can prevent its default behavior, which is useful for stopping the submission if there are errors in the fields.

Other Events

These events pertain to mouse and keyboard use and are especially relevant to form inputs.

focus

An element has *focus* when it can receive keyboard events. By default, the only elements that can receive focus are the document, links, and form inputs. Users typically change focus from one element to another by pressing the Tab key. The focus event does not bubble up the DOM tree.

You can make any element focusable by setting its tabindex attribute to 0. Then the user can tab to the element and control it with the keyboard.

blur

The blur event occurs when an element loses focus. Like the focus event, it does not bubble.

12

Libraries

Throughout this book you've seen helper functions for strings, arrays, elements, and events. You may want to use these or similar functions in your code. And when you start your second project, you may decide to copy much of this code over so you don't have to start from scratch. Ta-da! You've created a library!

The most important reason for using a library is to avoid reinventing the wheel for each project. JavaScript has a relatively small set of built-in functions, so collections of reusable code can be great time-savers.

JavaScript programmers also spend much of their time dealing with the differences between browsers, especially between Internet Explorer and all the other modern browsers like Firefox and Chrome. Sometimes it's a matter of different implementations, such as the standard addEventListener() and the nonstandard attachEvent(). Other times, a browser might completely lack a feature, such as querySelector(), and a library can fill that gap. The solution won't ever perform quite as well as the native function, but it's usually better than not having it at all.

A less important but very influential aspect of libraries has to do with coding style. JavaScript is an especially flexible language, and no two programmers write code exactly the same way. JavaScript libraries, however, tend to enforce a particular style. This can be through which language features they use, their naming conventions, or their design and organization. A unified style makes it easier to read similar code and work with other programmers.

Lastly, nearly every library is open source and free to use in your projects. This encourages innovation, and many developers release components and tools for use with the library. Using a library allows you to take advantage of the hard work of hundreds of other JavaScript programmers all over the world.

Choosing a Library

Dozens of JavaScript libraries are available. On the whole, anything you do in one library you can do just as well in another. So, how do you choose?

First, does the library do what you need to do? If you need complicated features, such as sophisticated data grids or drawing capabilities, you may want to consider certain libraries over others. If your needs are simple, most popular libraries will fit the bill.

Another consideration is if you need your library to play well with other code. In Chapter 6, you learned about adding methods to built-in prototypes and how that can possibly conflict with other code. Some libraries are built on augmenting `Array.prototype` and other built-in objects, while others keep all their functions and properties in a single namespace to avoid conflicts.

File size is an important consideration because the user will have to download the library along with your own code. A large library may have a lot of code that you don't even use but still makes your pages load slower. Fortunately, large libraries are getting smarter with lazy loading techniques, and companies such as Google and Yahoo! provide content distribution networks for many popular libraries.

In addition to the features provided by the library itself, you should consider what other code is available for your library. Maybe the library developers don't see a reason to include an image slideshow component in the library, but many other independent developers have probably created and released one that you can leverage. Take a look at the source code of third-party components for clearly written and well-commented code before deciding to use it on your sites.

Lastly and most importantly, choosing a JavaScript library is a matter of personal style. Some libraries will just make more sense to you in how they name functions and organize the code. In the end, you can achieve the same goals no matter what library you use, so pick one that feels right to you.

note Learning a library is like learning an entirely new language on top of JavaScript. This book obviously can't cover all the specifics of any one library. Instead, when a tutorial uses a library, it will include a short glossary at the end of the chapter that briefly explains the functions and concepts used.

In addition, you should use the online documentation available at each library's website, as well as the myriad of "cheat sheets" available online to learn more.

Using Libraries with This Book

Many of the tutorials in the following chapters use JavaScript libraries. You can download the libraries from their respective Web sites, but instead of making you do that, I'm including references to copies of the files stored by Google and Yahoo!

Google's Ajax Libraries API (*http://code.google.com/apis/ajaxlibs/*) is a content distribution network (CDN) that provides copies of recent versions of JavaScript library files. One downside to using Google's API or any other CDN is that you have to be connected to the Internet to continually download the files and test your code. If you want to follow the tutorials of this book offline, you'll need to download the libraries from their respective sites first.

YUI 3 uses some interesting techniques for including parts of the library, as I'll discuss in a moment. The easiest way to use the library is to use the Yahoo!'s own content distribution network.

I'm including the most recent versions of these libraries at the time of this writing. A newer version may be available by the time you're reading this, but sometimes changes in new versions will break your existing code. Use the version I've specified if you're running into problems.

You may notice that the source code I'm linking to is a big jumbled mess. JavaScript code is often compressed to make the file size smaller by removing unnecessary whitespace and making variable names shorter. You can access the uncompressed source from the library's Web site. Google's API can also provide uncompressed versions.

jQuery

http://www.jquery.com

jQuery is the most popular JavaScript library on the Web. Created by John Resig in 2006, it is a general-purpose library that emphasizes interacting with HTML elements. It is a single JavaScript file currently weighing 59KB.

For the last couple of years, I've used jQuery more than any other library. I appreciate that it's a relatively small library with a manageable number of functions and utilities.

Coding with jQuery

Using jQuery in your pages is quite simple; just include the entire library in your HTML document:

```
<script src="http://ajax.googleapis.com/ajax/libs/jquery/
➥ 1.4.1/jquery.min.js" type="text/javascript"></script>
<script type="text/javascript">
    (function($) {
        $("#myElement").addClass("jquery-fied");
    })(jQuery); // Self-invoking function
</script>
```

The entire library is stored on the jQuery variable, which is often aliased as $. Because $ is a common variable name in other libraries, it's a common practice to pass the jQuery variable as an argument in a self-invoking function and aliasing it yourself, as shown in the previous example.

You can also start your scripts by attaching a DOMContentLoaded event handler:

```
jQuery(document).ready(function() {
    // The DOM is ready
});
```

jQuery Objects

Most of jQuery's functionality involves finding, creating, and manipulating DOM elements. To make this simple and intuitive, it wraps DOM elements in *jQuery objects*, which are special arrays with added methods. (I discussed wrapping DOM elements in order to add methods in Chapter 10.)

You can make a jQuery object in three ways:

- Pass a DOM element to the jQuery function.

  ```
  var jQueryObject = $(document.getElementById("#myElement"));
  ```

- Pass a CSS selector to the jQuery function.

  ```
  var specialLinks = $("a.special");
  ```

- Pass an HTML string to the jQuery function to create a new node.

  ```
  var newParagraph = $('<p class="message">Message</p>');
  ```

You can act on a jQuery object the same regardless of whether it contains one element, many elements, or no elements at all.

```
// Add a class name for one element
jQueryObject.addClass("special");

// Change the class attribute for every element in the object
specialLinks.removeClass("special");

// This jQuery object contains no elements
var empty = $("#nonexistent");
```

```
empty.length;
0
empty.addClass("special"); // No effect
```

jQuery doesn't warn you that the object is empty before you call methods on it, so your script may fail silently.

You can chain multiple methods together to perform several operations in one line of code.

```
header.show("slow").find("span").addClass("active").
➥ click(onClick);
```

You can also create your own jQuery object methods by adding methods to $.fn.

```
$.fn.makeAwesome = function() {
    // Loop over each element in the object
    return this.each(function() {
        // Act upon each element. I wish
        // there really was an awesome attribute
        this.attr("awesome", true);
    });
};
$("#element").makeAwesome();
```

Most jQuery plug-ins and third-party components use this functionality to extend jQuery's capabilities.

jQuery Utilities

jQuery also includes a number of functions not directly related to DOM elements, including Ajax and array utilities. They are available as properties of the jQuery variable.

```
jQuery.ajax({
    url : "data.php",
    success : function(response) {
        console.log(response);
    }
});
```

jQuery UI

http://jqueryui.com/

jQuery also has a medium-sized component library called jQuery UI that contains support for drag-and-drop, sortables, tabs, progress bars, other effects such as "bounce" and "slide," and more. You can download a build of jQuery UI that contains only the components you need from the project's Web site.

YUI 3

http://developer.yahoo.com/yui/3/

Yahoo! is a mecca for JavaScript, and the company has put its knowledge and experience into creating the Yahoo! User Interface Library. Version 3, released in 2009, takes lessons learned from previous versions and other libraries to provide a well-organized, robust feature set.

Coding with YUI 3

YUI 3 has a large number of native components and a growing number of third-party components. It leverages lazy loading to speed up download times. The "seed" file is only 15KB and manages dependent files in a simple method call.

```
<script type="text/javascript" src="http://yui.yahooapis.com/
➡ combo?3.0.0/build/yui/yui-min.js"></script>
<script type="text/javascript">
    YUI().use("overlay", function(Y) {
        var overlay = new Y.Overlay();
    });
</script>
```

This example includes the seed file in one <script> element and uses the YUI().use() method to load all the JavaScript required to use the Overlay widget, which ends up being another 98KB. Using this pattern, you download only the code you need for each page, which helps avoid wasting bandwidth.

Once the rest of the JavaScript downloads, the library executes the callback function. The Y object contains all the methods and objects in the library for you to use in your code. Using callback functions like this encourages programmers to encapsulate their code in functions to avoid conflicts with other JavaScript in the page. The Y object is specific to that script and available only inside the callback function.

Once the callback function executes, YUI 3 operates similarly to jQuery; just replace $ with Y. It has basically the same support for CSS selectors, event handling, and chainability, just with different method names:

```
Y.one("#domId").all(".className").on("click", onClick);
```

YUI 3 stands apart from jQuery by having a large number of widgets and components built into the library itself, including the following:

- Plug-in and widget infrastructure that helps you organize your code
- Components such as drag and drop, style sheet utilities, and history and cookie management
- Widgets for overlays and slider controls

This makes the library much larger and more daunting to learn. Fortunately, the documentation, which you can find at *http://developer. yahoo.com/yui/3/api/*, is excellent.

YUI 3 Gallery

http://yuilibrary.com/gallery/

The YUI 3 Gallery is a great resource for finding a large number of components built by third-party developers for YUI 3. These range from user interface widgets such as accordions and date pickers to sophisticated utilities for Ajax and form validation.

MooTools

http://mootools.net/

MooTools arrived in 2006 alongside jQuery and many other libraries. It has many of the same capabilities as jQuery and YUI 3, but its authors took a different approach to organizing the code and providing features.

Coding with MooTools

You can include the entire MooTools Core library from Google's Ajax Libraries API:

```
<script src="http://ajax.googleapis.com/ajax/libs/
➡mootools/1.2.4/mootools-yui-compressed.js"
➡type="text/javascript"></script>
```

MooTools also gives you the ability to create a custom version of the library that includes only the functionality you need for your scripts. The MooTools Builder (*http://mootools.net/core*) has checkboxes for each component of the library if you desire a slimmer, more efficient library file.

MooTools also wraps DOM elements using a custom Element data type that provides additional methods and properties to facilitate finding, creating, and manipulating elements. MooTools contains many of the same element methods as jQuery, but it tends to use longer and argu-ably clearer method names.

The *http://mootorial.com/* Web site links to several great tutorials to get a feel for MooTools.

Namespacing

The biggest difference between MooTools and the libraries discussed earlier is in how it organizes its code. Unlike jQuery and YUI 3, MooTools spreads its properties and functions across several global variables, including $, $$, $A, Class, Element, Fx, and Request. It also adds methods to the prototypes of built-in objects such as Function and Array. Many programmers find this to be a clearer or more useful approach to library organization, but you do have to be more careful about conflicts between global variables.

MooTools More

http://mootools.net/more

The MooTools More library contains a number of plug-ins to the Core library for form and dragging functionality, additional effects, interface widgets, and internationalization and translation utilities. Like with the Core library, you can customize your library files to include only the plug-ins you need.

13

Image Slideshow

It's pretty amazing how many different ways you can hide and show page elements to create menus, tabs, accordions, and other custom user interface components. This chapter will show you how to create a simple slideshow of images, the core of which is elegantly hiding and showing one image at a time.

Debugging Your Code

This is the first chapter in the book that will walk you step-by-step through a nontrivial example. If you get stuck, Firebug will become your best friend. Here are some tips to help you debug your code:

- Check the console to see whether there are any errors. Firebug does a pretty good job of telling you on which line number the error occurred.

  If the error actually occurs inside a JavaScript library, Firebug's output might be a bit cryptic. Expand the error message by clicking the triangle to see what line number in your file is involved (**Figure 13.1**).

Figure 13.1
The error started on line 95 in slideshow.js.

- If you don't have any errors, check your variables to make sure they hold the values you expect. Use console.log() to print the value of the variables to the console. You may find that an array is actually empty or you have false instead of true.

- Firebug's Script tab is really powerful but takes some effort to understand. It allows you to add breakpoints to specific lines of code so you can stop the script and inspect the variables at that point.

- When in doubt, back up a few steps and make sure you typed everything correctly. Programming is not a forgiving endeavor.

Slideshow Ingredients

For this simple example, you need the following:

- A simple HTML page with the list of images (slideshow.html)

- A simple style sheet to help position and display the images and controls (slideshow.css)

- A handful of LOLcat images to test with (*http://www.lolcats.com*)

Figure 13.2 shows a preview of the final result.

Figure 13.2
*The LOLcat
slideshow
example.*

This list of functional requirements helps plan how you want the widget to behave:

- Without JavaScript, the page should contain the first image and a list of links to the subsequent images.

- The visible image should fade out as the next image fades in.

- The slideshow should loop back to the first image after showing the last image.

- The slideshow should automatically cycle through images every five seconds until the user clicks the next or previous arrows.

- Each image should be centered in the slideshow, regardless of size.

It would be much easier to create a slideshow for images that are all the same size. In fact, that last requirement almost doubles the length of the code. If I hadn't planned for it, I might have organized my code very differently, which is why it really helps to decide on your functionality in advance.

Slideshow HTML

This example HTML document contains only the bare-minimum markup to demonstrate how to build a slideshow:

```
<!DOCTYPE html>
<html class="no-js">
   <head>
      <title>LOLcat Slideshow</title>
      <link rel="stylesheet" href="slideshow.css"
      ➥type="text/css" />
      <script type="text/javascript">
         (function(d, c) { d[c] = d[c].replace(/\bno-js\b/,
         ➥"js"); })(document.documentElement, "className");
      </script>

   </head>
   <body>
      <div id="slideshow">
         <div class="slides">
```

```
            <img src="lolcat-1.jpg" width="450" height="336"
            ➡alt="Lolcat 1" />
        </div>
        <ul>
            <li><a href="lolcat-2.jpg" data-size="350x263">
            ➡Lolcat 2</a></li>
            <li><a href="lolcat-3.jpg" data-size="450x350">
            ➡Lolcat 3</a></li>
            <li><a href="lolcat-4.jpg" data-size="450x314">
            ➡Lolcat 4</a></li>
        </ul>
    </div>

    <script src="http://ajax.googleapis.com/ajax/libs/
    ➡jquery/1.4.1/jquery.min.js" type="text/javascript">
    ➡</script>
    <script src="slideshow.js" type="text/javascript">
    ➡</script>
  </body>
</html>
```

As short as the document is, you should notice several important details:

- The page links to a style sheet called slideshow.css that you'll create in a moment.

- The page also includes references to jQuery from the Google Libraries API and a new file called slideshow.js that you'll also create.

- The opening <html> tag and the first <script> element use the no-js/ js technique I described in Chapter 8.

- The slideshow is contained in a <div> with the ID of "slideshow," which makes it easy to hook JavaScript behavior into the page.

- Each image will exist inside the slides <div>, but I've included only the first image in the markup.

- The slideshow includes an unordered list of links that point to the remaining images. I've also stored their sizes on the custom data-size attributes.

note This is a somewhat rudimentary but valid example of progressive enhancement. The unordered list of links serves dual purposes: Users without JavaScript can still access the remaining images by clicking the links and loading the images individually, and it's easy to use the data stored in the markup to build the slideshow dynamically. I consider it a small victory whenever I can reuse accessible markup in the page to create a more engaging experience for users who can support it.

Slideshow CSS

Create a file called slideshow.css, and include the following CSS rules. It's pretty bare now, but you'll add more rules to support the JavaScript behavior in the next section.

```
#slideshow .slides {
    position: relative;
    margin: 0 auto;
    width: 450px;
}

html.js #slideshow .slides img {
    position: absolute;
}
```

I prefixed the second selector with html.js because I want the images to be absolutely positioned only if JavaScript is available to create the slideshow.

Slideshow JavaScript

Since you already know all the functional requirements of slideshow, you can quickly sketch an outline of the JavaScript code using comments. Create a file called slideshow.js, and enter this code:

```
(function($) {

    // Include utility jQuery plug-ins
    // Declare initial variables
    // Create images from the link list
    // Collect all images in one node set and hide the list
    // Resize slides <div> to hold the largest images
    // Center each image
    // Save a reference to the first image
    // The function to show the next or previous image
    // Start timer to cycle through images
    // Create next and previous controls
    // The event handler for the controls

})(jQuery); // Self-invoking function executes automatically
```

Including all the code in a self-invoking function lets you declare functions and variables without worrying that another script might overwrite them and cause conflicts.

Skipping the "Include utility jQuery plug-ins" comment for now, add this code beneath the "Declare initial variables" line:

```
var slideshow = $("#slideshow");
var slides = slideshow.find(".slides");
var currentImageIndex = 0;
```

The first thing you need to do is find the slideshow <div> by passing a CSS selector to the jQuery function ($()). Store it on a variable so that you can find other elements inside it later in the script. The first element to find is the slides <div>. You'll also need to keep track of the currently visible image with the currentImageIndex variable.

Best Practices for Using CSS Selectors in JavaScript

There's only one <div class="slides"> element in the page, so why did I use slideshow.find(".slides") instead of just $(".slides")?

Internet Explorer as well as older browsers do not support getElementsByClassName() and querySelectorAll(). JavaScript libraries provide support for these utilities in older browsers by looping over every element to find the ones that match your class name or CSS selector. This can take a noticeable amount of time if the library has to loop over many elements.

By using slideshow.find(), you can limit the search to just the elements inside the slideshow <div> to improve the performance of your code.

Creating the Slideshow Images

The next step is to use the list of links to create images and add them to the slideshow.

```
// Create images from the link list
slideshow.find("ul a").each(function() {
    var link = $(this);
    var size = link.attr("data-size").split("x");
```

```
    $("<img />").attr({
        src : link.attr("href"),
        width : size[0],
        height : size[1],
        alt : link.text()
    }).hide().appendTo(slides);
});
```

This code snippet might look a little daunting because jQuery allows you to do so much in very little code.

The first thing it does is find all the links in the unordered list using find() and loop over them using the each() function. jQuery encourages a functional coding style, meaning that you use looping functions such as each() more often than language features such as for or while.

Inside the loop function, you can access each link with the this keyword and turn it into a jQuery object by passing it to $(). Save it on the link variable because you'll access it three times in the loop function.

Each link has a string like "350x263" stored on the data-size attribute. It's easy to separate the width from the height by splitting on the "x."

When you pass an HTML string to the jQuery function, such as $("<img />"), it creates new HTML elements. The attr() method lets you pass attributes to the new element, which is how you can set the src, width, height, and alt attributes for each new image.

jQuery emphasizes *chainability*, allowing you to immediately call hide() and appendTo() on the newly created <img> without having to save it to a variable first. The hide() method sets its display style property to "none," and the appendTo() method inserts it into the slides <div>.

It's very easy to write ten lines of code in jQuery that require six paragraphs to explain. I happen to enjoy jQuery's terse style, but it's definitely a matter of personal preference.

Now that you've created all the images, create an array that holds all of them (including the one that existed in the markup).

```
// Collect all images in one node set and hide the list
var images = slides.find("img");
slideshow.find("ul").hide();
```

Centering the Images

To center each of these arbitrarily sized images, you need to find the tallest and widest dimensions. This is something I do often enough that I've written some jQuery plug-ins to make this easy. You have to include plug-ins before they are used in your scripts. Skip to the top of your JavaScript file, and add this code:

```
// Include utility jQuery plug-ins
$.fn.tallest = function(outer, margins) {
    var fn = outer ? "height" : "outerHeight";
    return Math.max.apply(Math, $.map(this, function(el) {
        return $(el)[fn](margins);
    }));
};

$.fn.widest = function(outer, margins) {
    var fn = outer ? "width" : "outerWidth";
    return Math.max.apply(Math, $.map(this, function(el) {
        return $(el)[fn](margins);
    }));
};
```

Back toward the bottom of your JavaScript file, you can now use the
tallest() and widest() methods to set the size of the slides <div> to
hold the largest images.

```
// Resize slides <div> to hold the largest images
var slidesWidth = images.widest();
var slidesHeight = images.tallest();
slides.css({
   width : slidesWidth,
   height : slidesHeight
});
```

The css() method is a shorthand way of setting style properties on
elements. It takes care of adding "px" to numbers for you and other small
conveniences.

```
// Center each image
images.each(function() {
   var image = $(this);
   image.css({
      left : slidesHeight / 2 - image.width() / 2,
      top : slidesHeight / 2 - image.height() / 2
   });
});
```

Centering elements with JavaScript is a pretty common task. I find myself
typing variations of this formula quite often. The each() method makes
it easy to set the left and top style properties for every image.

```
// Save a reference to the first image
var activeImage = images.eq(currentImageIndex);
```

Before you start the slideshow, you'll need to save a reference to the first
image. The eq() method returns a single element wrapped in a jQuery

object. (If you wanted just the plain DOM element, you can access it as an element in an array: images[0].)

The Slideshow Code

Everything up to this point has been setup code. The meat of the script is in the showImage() function, which takes an index that indicates which image to show.

```
// The function to show the next or previous image
function showImage(newIndex) {
    currentImageIndex = newIndex >= images.length ? 0 :
    ➥ newIndex;
    currentImageIndex = currentImageIndex < 0 ? images.length
    ➥ - 1 : currentImageIndex;

    activeImage.fadeOut();
    activeImage = images.eq(currentImageIndex).fadeIn();
}
```

The first two lines are another pattern I end up writing a lot. There are only four images (indices 0 through 3), so when you pass 4 to showImage(), the number should wrap around to 0. Likewise, if you pass -1, it should wrap the other direction to 3. At this point, I can easily recognize this pattern when I see it, but you may prefer a more obvious version.

```
// This example code doesn't go in slideshow.js
currentImageIndex = newIndex;
if (currentImageIndex >= images.length) {
    currentImageIndex = 0;
} else if (currentImageIndex < 0) {
    currentImageIndex = images.length - 1;
}
```

To actually cross-fade the images, jQuery provides two very useful animation functions, `fadeIn()` and `fadeOut()`. To hide the current image, simply call `fadeOut()` on the image stored on the `activeImage` variable.

To show the next image, retrieve it from the `images` collection with the `eq()` method and call `fadeIn()`. Also be sure to save this image on the `activeImage` variable for the next time you call the `showImage()` function.

The last thing you need to do to get the slideshow running is to call `showImage()` repeatedly using `setInterval()`.

```
// Start timer to cycle through images
var interval = setInterval(function() {
    showImage(currentImageIndex + 1);
}, 5000);
```

Each time `setInterval()` calls this anonymous function, it calls on `showImage()` to display the next image by adding one to `currentImageIndex`. You'll also need to save a reference to the interval to be able to cancel the automatic image rotation.

Slideshow Controls

I try not to mix HTML into my JavaScript files, but I make an exception for HTML elements that would have no use without JavaScript. You could have put these links in the HTML document and retrieved them with CSS selectors. However, I think creating these elements with JavaScript is the appropriate solution in this case.

```
// Create next and previous controls
$('<a href="#" class="next">\u232A</a>').appendTo(slides).
➥bind("click", +1, onClick);
$('<a href="#" class="prev">\u2329</a>').appendTo(slides).
➥bind("click", -1, onClick);
```

The Unicode entities (such as "\u232A") in the text of these links are nice-looking arrow characters pointing left and right.

This is another example of passing an HTML string to the jQuery function to create a new element. Again, you can immediately append the elements to the page and add event handlers by chaining jQuery methods.

The bind() method is jQuery's version of addEventListener()—another advantage with JavaScript libraries are the shorter names—but with a few differences. You can optionally pass some data to the event handler in the second argument. You're using the same event handler for both links and passing in +1 or -1 to indicate which direction to cycle the slideshow.

The event handler, onClick(), is very simple because it passes on the real functionality to the showImages() function.

```
// Event handler for the controls
function onClick(event) {
    event.preventDefault();
    clearInterval(interval);
    showImage(currentImageIndex + event.data);
}
```

The first thing the event handler does is prevent the default link behavior with event.preventDefault(). jQuery normalizes the event object across all browsers so you can use the standard API even in Internet Explorer.

The handler then clears the interval so that the slideshow no longer automatically cycles after the user interacts with it.

Lastly, it calls showImage() very much like the function passed to setInterval() does. jQuery stores the extra data passed to bind() on the event.data property, so the index passed to showImage() corresponds to the clicked link.

Finally, even though you created the links with JavaScript, it's usually best to style them in CSS. Add these rules to position the next and previous links to the left and right of the slideshow.

```css
#slideshow .next,
#slideshow .prev {
    position: absolute;
    top: 50%;
    margin-top: -0.5em;
    width: 40px;
    font-size: 32px;
    text-decoration: none;
}

#slideshow .next {
    right: -50px;
    padding-left: 10px;
}

#slideshow .prev {
    left: -50px;
    padding-right: 10px;
    text-align: right;
}
```

jQuery Glossary

Here is a short summary of the jQuery functions and concepts used in this chapter. You can find much more information in the online documentation at *http://api.jquery.com/*.

The jQuery Function: $()

This remarkable little function has multiple uses.

- It finds elements if you pass it a CSS selector.

  ```
  var foundElements = $("#domId > .selector + div");
  ```

- It adds methods to DOM elements by wrapping them in jQuery objects. This is especially useful inside iterators and event handlers.

  ```
  var wrappedElement = $(this);
  wrappedElement.fadeIn();
  ```

- It creates DOM elements if you pass it an HTML string.

  ```
  var newElement = $('<a href="index.html">Click here</a>');
  ```

jQuery Object Methods

jQuery objects provide dozens of methods for finding, creating, and manipulating DOM elements. Like the jQuery function ($()), many of these methods have multiple uses, so these descriptions are incomplete. These methods act upon single elements and collections of elements in the same manner.

find(selector) Finds child elements that match the given selector.

attr(name[, *value*]) Reads an attribute from the first element in the set and sets attributes on all the elements.

hide() Sets the display style property to "none."

appendTo(parent) Appends the element to the parent node.

css(name[, value]), css(object) Reads and sets the style properties of the element(s). You can pass the name and value or an object containing several name/value pairs.

width([value]) Reads and sets the width of the element(s).

height([value]) Reads and sets the height of the element(s).

each(func) Calls the given function for each element in the collection.

eq(index) Returns a jQuery object containing the single element at the given index in the collection.

fadeOut() Animates the element's opacity to zero and sets the display style property to "none."

fadeIn() Animates the element's opacity to one.

bind(eventType[, data], handler) jQuery's version of addEventListener(). It can optionally pass data to the handler function in the Event object.

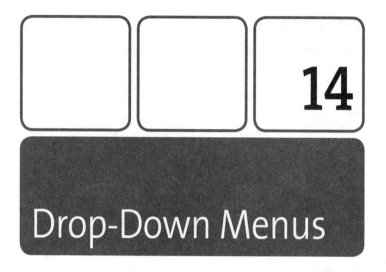

14

Drop-Down Menus

Drop-down menus are ubiquitous on computers, both in desktop software and on the Web. They can be useful tools for organizing the hierarchy of a complex Web site by hiding deeper pages in submenus until the user needs them. This chapter demonstrates how to build a simple menu system using the MooTools JavaScript library.

Menu HTML

The basic HTML document should be fairly unsurprising if you've read the previous example chapter.

```
<!DOCTYPE html>
<html class="no-js">
    <head>
        <title>Menu</title>
        <link rel="stylesheet" href="menu.css" type="text/css" />
        <script type="text/javascript">
            (function(d, c) { d[c] = d[c].replace(/\bno-js\b/,
            ➥"js"); })(document.documentElement, "className");
        </script>

    </head>
    <body>
        <!-- Menu Markup Goes Here -->

        <script src="http://ajax.googleapis.com/ajax/libs/
        ➥mootools/1.2.4/mootools-yui-compressed.js" type="text/
        ➥javascript"></script>
        <script src="menu.js" type="text/javascript"></script>
    </body>
</html>
```

It includes two important details to notice:

- The <html> tag has a class name called no-js, which you'll use for fallback behavior in the CSS.

- The first <script> element loads the MooTools library from Google's JavaScript library API. The second loads a file called menu.js, which you'll create in a moment. (The file doesn't include the YUI library, by the way, but instead uses the YUI Compressor to make the file smaller.)

Menu Markup

Menus and navigation elements are commonly marked up as unordered lists of links. For a complex menu hierarchy, you can simply nest unordered lists inside list items. Replace the <!-- Menu Markup Goes Here --> comment shown earlier with this basic markup for the menu example:

```
<div id="menu">
   <ul>
      <li><a href="#">File</a>
         <ul>
            <li><a href="#">New</a></li>
            <li><a href="#">Save</a></li>
            <li><a href="#">Close</a></li>
         </ul>
      </li>
      <li><a href="#">Edit</a>
         <ul>
            <li><a href="#">Cut</a></li>
            <li><a href="#">Copy</a></li>
            <li><a href="#">Paste</a></li>
         </ul>
      </li>
      <li><a href="#">Window</a>
         <ul>
            <li><a href="#">Minimize</a></li>
            <li><a href="#">Zoom</a></li>
            <li><a href="#">Fire Missiles</a></li>
         </ul>
```

(continues on next page)

```
      </li>
   </ul>
</div>
```

Menu CSS

This simple CSS is in no way the most attractive way to style a drop-down menu, but it demonstrates the basics. Create a file called menu.css, and add this code:

```css
/* Remove the default list styles */
ul, ul li {
   margin: 0;
   padding: 0;
   list-style: none outside;
}

/* Horizontal menu items */
#menu li {
   position: relative;
   float: left;
}

#menu li a {
   padding: 4px 10px;
   background: #ddd;
   display: block;
}
```

```
#menu li.open a {
   background: #aaa;
}

/* Submenus are aligned to the left edge of their parents */
#menu li ul {
   position: absolute;
   display: none;
   left: 0;
}

#menu li li {
   float: none;
   white-space: nowrap;
   zoom: 1; /* force hasLayout in IE */
}

/* IE needs a little help displaying submenu links */
#menu li li a {
   zoom: 1;
   _width: 100%; /* Hack to affect only IE6 */
}
```

Progressive Enhancement

You can actually create a simple drop-down menu with just HTML and
CSS. Add this CSS declaration to menu.css to see how:

```
#menu li:hover ul {
   display: block;
}
```

Now when you hover over a menu item, the display style of the submenu changes to block, and the menu appears (**Figure 14.1**). Your job is done; take the rest of the day off.

Figure 14.1
The drop-down menu works with just CSS.

Not really, of course. Even though this CSS-only solution is great, you might want to add some JavaScript for various reasons:

- Internet Explorer 6 doesn't understand the :hover pseudoselector on elements other than <a>, so this solution doesn't work for users with that browser.

- Using :hover doesn't provide the most usable experience. The submenu appears and disappears immediately, so it's easy to accidentally move the mouse too far or too fast and miss your target. You can add a short delay with JavaScript to mitigate this. Also, you can't trigger the submenu with the keyboard.

- You might want to show and hide the submenus by clicking the menu items or some other behavior. The example in this chapter takes this approach.

It's a good idea to leave in the CSS-only solution even if you provide JavaScript behavior for menus, just in case the user doesn't have JavaScript enabled. But you'll want to disable this CSS so that it doesn't conflict with your JavaScript solution by using the .no-js:

```
html.no-js #menu li:hover ul {
    display: block;
}
```

Menu JavaScript

The MooTools library places a lot of emphasis on creating "classes" to organize code. It provides a data type called Class, which has some special functionality to emulate classical object-oriented patterns such as inheritance and composition. Classes are one of many ways to organize your code. They have some downsides, which will become clear in this example, but they also allow for code that is easy to read and understand, especially if you're used to other object-oriented languages.

> **note** If you want to learn more about classical inheritance and composition, I recommend searching the Web for tutorials on object-oriented patterns in ActionScript 3. JavaScript and ActionScript 3 are similar languages, but the latter includes language features for more structured object-oriented programming.

Create a file called menu.js to start creating your Menu class. The basic structure of the class looks like this:

```
var Menu = new Class({
    initialize : function(container) {},
    initMenuItems : function() {},
    addMouseBehavior : function() {},
    onClick : function(event) {},
    toggleLink : function(link) {},
    closeLink : function(link) {},
    openLink : function(link) {},
    showMenu : function(submenu) {},          (continues on next page)
```

```
    hideMenu : function(submenu) {},
    closeOtherLinks : function(currentLink) {},
    onOutsideClick : function(event) {}
});
```

The Class constructor function takes an object that defines all the
properties and methods for instances of this class. At its core, the Class
constructor just creates a new data type and adds these properties to its
prototype, as you learned to do in Chapter 6.

MooTools Constructor Functions

MooTools classes use the initialize() method as a constructor function. It's called automatically when you create a new instance with the
new keyword.

```
initialize : function(container) {
    this.container = container;
    this.initMenuItems();
    this.addMouseBehavior();
},
```

This constructor method simply saves a reference to the menu element
and executes other methods to add the menu's functionality.

Add this code at the top of menu.js to create the menu once the document loads. MooTools provides the custom domready event on the
window element that simulates the DOMContentLoaded event. The $()
function finds an element by its ID.

```
window.addEvent("domready", function() {
    var menu = new Menu($("menu"));
});
```

Arrays in MooTools

The next method, initMenuItems(), finds all the elements in the menu's container that you'll need to add menu behavior.

```
initMenuItems : function() {
    // The top <ul>
    this.list = this.container.getChildren();
    // The top <li>s (File, Edit, Window)
    this.items = $$(this.list.getChildren());
    // The links in the top <li>s
    this.links = $$(this.list.getElements("a"));
    // The submenu <ul>s
    this.submenus = this.container.getElements("ul ul");
},
```

MooTool's element-finding methods, such as getChildren() and getElements(), return special arrays with added methods. When you call an element-finding method on an array of MooTools objects, it returns an array of arrays:

```
// An array of links for each item in this.items
this.items.getChildren("a")
[[a #], [a #], [a #]]
```

The $$() function has many uses, one of which is flattening these nested arrays for use with all the MooTools methods.

```
$$(this.items.getChildren("a"))
[a #, a #, a #]
```

Event Handlers in MooTools Classes

The Menu class's addMouseEvents() method adds click event handlers to the links in the menu and on the document element.

```
addMouseBehavior : function() {
    this.links.addEvent("click", this.onClick.bind(this));
    $(document).addEvent("click", this.onOutsideClick.bind(this));
},
```

The onClick() method is very simple. It passes the clicked element to
the toggleLink() method and prevents the event's default behavior to
keep the browser from navigating to a new page.

```
onClick : function(event) {
    this.toggleLink(event.target);
    event.preventDefault();
},
```

Practical Function Context Binding

The onClick() function is a method belonging to a Menu object. But
you're also using it as an event handler. You need access to two different objects inside the onClick() event handler:

- The current Menu object so that you have access to other properties and methods defined by the Menu class

- The clicked element so that you know which submenu to open

You learned in Chapter 11 that event handlers execute in the context
of the element handling the event. Under normal circumstances, you
could access the clicked element with the this keyword:

```
this.links.addEvent("click", this.onClick);
onClick : function(event) {
    // Open or close the submenu for this link
    var clickedLink = this;
    ???.toggleLink(clickedLink);
}
```

(continues on next page)

Practical Function Context Binding (continued)

This won't work, however, because toggleLink() also a Menu object method. Since the this keyword refers to the clicked element, you don't have access to the toggleLink() method for the current Menu object. Fortunately, MooTools provides a helper method for all functions to bind the context of a function to an object:

```
this.links.addEvent("click", this.onClick.bind(this));
onClick : function(event) {
    // Open or close the submenu for this link
    var clickedLink = ???;
    this.toggleLink(clickedLink);
}
```

Now you need another way to access the clicked element, since you changed what the this keyword referred to. In this case, the clicked element is also available as event.target.

```
onClick : function(event) {
    // Open or close the submenu for this link
    var clickedLink = event.target;
    this.toggleLink(clickedLink);
}
```

If the link contained children, you might have had to walk up the DOM tree to get to the link element because of event bubbling.

If you're used to programming in a language with built-in classes, this context binding mess might seem like an awkward step. In ActionScript 3, for instance, the this keyword *always* refers to the current object and always has access to the object's properties and methods. It's easier to change function context in JavaScript, so these extra steps are necessary if you want to emulate classes and classical object-oriented patterns.

Showing and Hiding Submenus

The behavior of this menu isn't too complicated. When the user clicks a menu item, the following happens:

- If the item's submenu is closed, open it after closing any other open submenus.

- If the item's submenu is open, close it.

Also, when the user clicks anywhere other than the menu, it should close any open submenus. That's why you're binding a click event to the <body> element.

```
toggleLink : function(link) {
    if (link.retrieve("open")) {
        this.closeLink(link);
    } else {
        this.openLink(link);
    }
},
```

An easy way to keep track of the status of a link and its submenu is using MooTool's store() and retrieve() methods, which allow you to store arbitrary data on an object. If the "open" data for a link is true, call the closeLink() method. Otherwise, call the openLink() method.

```
closeLink : function(link) {
    var submenu = link.getParent().getElements("ul");
    if (submenu.length) {
        link.store("open", false);
        link.getParent().removeClass("open");
        this.hideMenu(submenu);
    }
},
```

```
openLink : function(link) {
    var submenu = link.getParent().getElements("ul");
    if (submenu.length) {
        link.store("open", true);
        link.getParent().addClass("open");
        this.showMenu(submenu);
        this.closeOtherLinks(link);
    }
},
```

These two methods are nearly identical. They perform the following tasks:

- Find the appropriate submenu for the clicked link. Make sure the submenu exists (the array returned by getElements() has a length greater than 0).

- Set the "open" data to true or false appropriately.

- Add or remove the "open" CSS class to the containing <li>.

- Show or hide the submenu.

- For openLink() only, close any other open submenus.

To find the submenu for a link, traverse up the DOM tree to its parent <li> element with getParent(), and look for any <ul> elements inside it.

To show or hide a submenu, simply set the display style of the <ul> to "block" or "none," just like the CSS-only implementation shown earlier.

```
showMenu : function(submenu) {
    submenu.setStyle("display", "block");
},

hideMenu : function(submenu) {
    submenu.setStyle("display", "none");
},
```

> **note** It may seem like overkill to create entirely separate methods to run a single line of code, but it will become clear why I structured the code this way when you extend the Menu class later in the chapter.

Closing any other open submenus is pretty simple: Just call the closeLink() method for all the other links.

```
closeOtherLinks : function(currentLink) {
    var otherLinks = $A(this.links).erase(currentLink);
    otherLinks.each(this.closeLink, this);
},
```

The $A() function is a MooTools helper that adds useful methods to an array. The method you want here is erase(), which removes the given item from the array.

The each() method runs a function for each item in an array, but just like with event handlers, you must make sure that this.closeLink() executes in the context of the Menu object. Fortunately, you can pass a context object as the second argument in each().

Clicking Outside the Menus

The final method in the Menu class is the event handler for the click event on the <body> element. Recall from Chapter 11 that click events bubble up the DOM tree all the way to the document, so you need to check to see whether the click event originated from an element inside the menu's container.

```
onOutsideClick : function(event) {
    if (! $(event.target).getParents().contains(this.
    ↪container)) {
        this.closeOtherLinks();
    }
}
```

MooTool's getParents() method returns every ancestor in the DOM tree for a particular element, so all you need to do is determine whether the menu's container exists in that array. If the click did not originate from inside the menu, you can close all the submenus by calling closeOtherLinks() without an argument.

Extending the Menu Class

Your drop-down menu should now work as expected, but it's not terribly exciting at this point. In this section you'll learn how to take advantage of the special functionality in MooTool's classes to add a fancy slide effect to the menu.

The slide effect is an extra component in MooTool's More library. Google's JavaScript libraries API doesn't provide this component, so you'll need to download it from the MooTool's Web site (*http://mootools.net/more*). Select the Fx.Slide box, and click Download at the bottom of the page. Include the downloaded JavaScript file after the core MooTools library in your HTML document.

```
<script src="http://ajax.googleapis.com/ajax/libs/mootools/
➥1.2.4/mootools-yui-compressed.js" type="text/javascript">
➥</script>
<script src="mootools-1.2.4.2-more.js" type="text/javascript">
➥</script>
<script src="menu.js" type="text/javascript"></script>
```

Instead of changing your Menu class to add the new functionality, you can create a new class that "extends" the Menu class. This new class, FancyMenu, inherits all the properties and methods of the Menu class. It can also selectively override Menu properties to add behavior specific to FancyMenu objects.

The basic structure of the FancyMenu class is much simpler than Menu. Because it inherits all the properties of the Menu class, you don't have to repeat methods such as initMenuItems() and addMouseBehavior(). Make sure this code comes *after* the Menu class in menu.js.

```
var FancyMenu = new Class({
    Extends : Menu,
    Implements : Options,

    options : {
        duration: "short"
    },

    initialize : function(container, options) {},
    addEffect : function(menu) {},
    showMenu : function(menu) {},
    hideMenu : function(menu) {}
});
```

The special Extends property tells MooTool's Class constructor that this new class will inherit properties from Menu.

The special Implements property pulls in some extra functionality from the MooTools Options component, which you'll use to make the FancyMenu behavior customizable. The default options for each FancyMenu object are stored on the options property by convention.

Change the domready event handler to use your new class:

```
window.addEvent("domready", function() {
    // var menu = new Menu($("menu"));
    var menu = new FancyMenu($("menu"));
});
```

Overriding Inherited Methods

The FancyMenu initialize() method should perform the same actions as the Menu initialize() method, with two additions:

- It should handle any customization passed in with the options argument.

- It should set up the slide effects for each submenu.

MooTools allows you to add behavior to an inherited method by overriding it and executing the original behavior with the special parent() method.

```
initialize : function(container, options) {
    this.setOptions(options || {});
    this.parent(container);
    this.submenus.each(this.addEffect, this);
},
```

The first line uses the setOptions() method. You don't have to define that method yourself; it's available from the Options component included by the Implements class property.

The second line calls the Menu initialize() method via the parent() method, which ensures that initMenuItems() and addMouseBehavior() are still executed.

The last line runs the new addEffect() method for each submenu.

Using MooTools Effects

MooTools provides the slide effect as a class called Fx.Slide. To use it, you create a new instance of the class, passing in the element that receives the effect and any optional parameters.

```
// This example code doesn't go in menu.js
var slideEffect = new Fx.Slide(submenu, {
   duration: "short"
});
```

You can then control the effect by calling methods such as show(),
hide(), slideIn(), slideOut(), and cancel().

```
// This example code doesn't go in menu.js
slideEffect.hide(); // Start hidden
slideEffect.slideIn(); // Slide the submenu into view
```

The effect works by wrapping the submenu <ul> in a <div> element with
its overflow style set to "hidden."

Because the slide effect adds a new element to the markup, you need to
add a little more CSS to menu.css to position it correctly.

```
#menu li div {
   position: absolute;
   left: 0;
}

#menu li div ul {
   position: relative;
}
```

The addEffect() method creates Fx.Slide objects for each submenu and
calls hide() to set their initial position. It uses the duration property
from the options object to determine the speed of the slide effect. Finally,
it stores the Fx objects for later use when the user clicks a menu item.

```
addEffect : function(submenu) {
   submenu.setStyle("display", "block");
```

```
    var slideEffect = new Fx.Slide(submenu, {
        duration: this.options.duration
    });
    slideEffect.hide();
    submenu.store("slide", slideEffect);
},
```

The final step is to override the showMenu() and hideMenu() methods to use the slide effect objects instead of just setting the display style.

```
showMenu : function(submenu) {
    submenu[0].retrieve("slide").cancel().slideIn();
},

hideMenu : function(submenu) {
    submenu[0].retrieve("slide").cancel().slideOut();
}
```

These methods retrieve the slide object from the stored data, cancel any currently active animations, and call slideIn() or slideOut() appropriately.

Because you implemented the MooTools Options component, you can customize the speed of the slide effect when creating the FancyMenu object.

```
var menu = new FancyMenu($("menu"), {
    duration : 1000 // One second in milliseconds
});
```

Now you have two different classes that define drop-down menu behavior, but you didn't have to write any code twice. If you don't mind the extra work managing method context and the this keyword for event listeners, MooTools classes and similar object-oriented patterns can be a great way to organize your code.

Keyboard Support

The Menu and FancyMenu classes support keyboard navigation pretty successfully because the click event responds to the Enter/Return key as well as the mouse. You can test this by navigating the links in the page with the Tab key.

The FancyMenu has a slight complication, though: Because of how the slide effect hides the submenus, you can still tab to their links even when they are hidden. Keyboard users prefer being able to tab only to visible elements. (The Menu class hides submenus with the display style property, so you can't tab to them.)

You can set the "tabability" of an element with the tabindex property. A tabindex of 0 means it can be tabbed to. A tabindex of -1 removes its "tabability."

MooTool's makes setting the tabindex property on all the links in a submenu a simple one-liner:

```
$$(submenu.getElements("a")).set("tabindex", -1);
```

Add this line to addEffect(), hideMenu(), and showMenu() to set the tabindex properties appropriately for hidden and visible submenus. Don't forget to change the -1 to a 0 in showMenu().

Now when you tab to a menu item, you have to hit Enter/Return to be able to tab to the links in its submenu.

MooTools Glossary

Here is a short summary of the MooTools functions used in this chapter. You can find much more information in the online documentation at *http://mootools.net/docs/core*.

Element Utilities

$(id) MooTool's version of getElementsById(). This returns a MooTools element that provides element methods.

$$(selector) Retrieves elements that match the given selector.

$$(collection) Returns an array of MooTools elements that each provides element methods.

Element Methods

element.addEvent(eventType, handler) MooTool's version of addEventListener().

element.getChildren() Returns the element's child elements.

element.getParent() Returns the element's parent element.

element.getParents() Returns an array of all of the element's ancestors.

element.store(name, value) Stores an arbitrary value on an element.

element.retrieve(name) Retrieves arbitrary values saved on the element with store().

element.setStyle(name, value) Sets the style property of the element(s).

element.set(name, value) Sets an attribute on the element(s).

element.addClass(className) Adds a class name to the element(s).

Array Utilities

$A(collection) Returns a true array from the given collection.

array.each(func) Calls the given function for each element in the array.

array.erase(value) Removes the given value from the array.

array.contains(value) Returns true if the array contains the given value.

Function Utilities

func.bind(context) Returns a new function that calls the function in the given context. This is similar to `bindContext()` from Chapter 5.

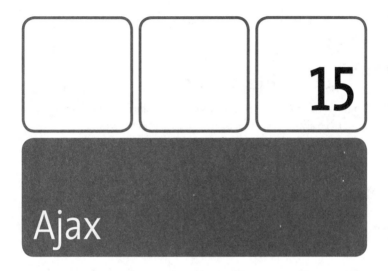

15

Ajax

Ajax used to be an acronym for "Asynchronous JavaScript and XML," but now it's just a buzzword for highly dynamic Web pages. With Ajax, you have the ability to send and receive data from your server without having to load a whole new page. This allows you to do the following:

- Quickly load additional content only when the user needs it, making your initial page load smaller
- Send data from links and forms back to the server without a page refresh, which makes your pages feel faster

The XMLHttpRequest object makes Ajax possible. Originally a Microsoft innovation, all modern browsers support it without too many cross-browser inconsistencies. I recommend researching how to use the native XMLHttpRequest object to understand what's going on under the hood, but for this tutorial, you'll just use jQuery's `$.ajax()` function to keep things simple.

Ajax Considerations

On the surface, Ajax is a relatively simple technique, but in practice you need to be aware of some security and usability concerns.

Servers

You'll need a server to use Ajax because browsers won't let JavaScript read files off your hard drive. This is an important security restriction; you never want to allow a script to access your important documents.

Same-Origin Policy

The same-origin policy is another security restriction that prevents a script from sending and receiving data from another server. It's especially important for Web pages that use cookies to manage user accounts. Without this restriction, a script could use your cookies and pretend to be you on another site.

Data Formats

Ajax responses are always text, but you have a few options on how that text is formatted.

Text or HTML. If the server responds with text or HTML, you can simply inject it into your HTML to add or update content on your page. Text responses can also provide arbitrary data such as error messages.

XML. The *X* in Ajax originally stood for XML, which was the common response type when Microsoft invented the XMLHttpRequest object. You

can use DOM methods and properties such as getElementsByTagName()
or childNodes to walk the XML DOM tree and extract information.
I think that using XML responses is overly complicated, so I avoid it when
possible.

JSON. JavaScript Object Notation (JSON) is a way to store data in a string
that looks like a JavaScript object or array. It's easy to turn this string into
a real JavaScript object, so it's my preferred data format in most Ajax
situations.

Modern browsers such as Firefox and Safari provide a simple API for
handling JSON:

```
JSON.stringify({ propertyName : "value" });
"{"propertyName":"value"}"
JSON.parse("{\"propertyName\":\"value\"}");
Object { propertyName="value"}
```

JavaScript libraries provide functions such as jQuery's $.parseJSON() so
that you can effortlessly handle JSON across all browsers.

User Experience

Users are used to loading new pages when they click links and submit
forms. If you replace that behavior with Ajax, you may need to do some
extra work so that users still know what's happening.

Loading indicators. The browser doesn't tell the user that you're making
an Ajax request. You should show some kind of loading indicator so the
user knows that something is happening. I like using animated GIFs, such
as the free ones at *http://www.ajaxload.info/*.

Back buttons and bookmarks. Ajax actions don't change the URL in the
browser's location field. This has two effects: The user can't bookmark

or share a URL that corresponds to your page's current state, and the browser's back and forward buttons are no longer useful. The solution is to use the `window.location.hash` property to change the URL without reloading the page.

- Before clicking an Ajax-driven link: `http://example.com/index.html`

- After clicking the link: `http://example.com/index.html#page2`

This is a complicated technique, so I'll skip this concern in the example later in the chapter. Check out the SWFAddress library (*http://www.asual. com/swfaddress/*) to learn more about this technique.

Accessibility and search engine optimization. Search engines and users without JavaScript enabled won't see your Ajax behaviors. It's always a great idea to use progressive enhancement so that your pages work just as well with and without Ajax. The following example demonstrates one way to achieve this.

Ajax Example

This example shows you how to take a simple Web page and add Ajax behavior to it. The page does three things:

- Shows a table of data pulled from a storage file

- Breaks the data into "pages" that you can navigate with Previous and Next links

- Provides a form for adding new data to the storage file

Ajax isn't much use unless your server can send and receive useful data, so you'll use a little bit of PHP (*http://php.net*) to manage your data. You'll need PHP version 5.2.0 or higher to use the JSON functions.

Servers and PHP

If you don't already have a server that supports PHP, I recommend installing the basic version of XAMPP (*http://www.apachefriends. org/en/xampp.html*). The installation instructions are excellent and should get you up and running fairly quickly. After you install XAMPP and start the Apache Web server, create your example files in these directories (assuming you installed it in the default location):

Windows: C:\xampp\htdocs

Mac: /Applications/XAMPP/htdocs/

Then you can point your browser to *http://localhost* to see your files.

Setup

This example has several interlocking parts, so you should keep them in separate files to make the code clearer. Start by creating these four files:

- index.php (XAMPP might supply this file for you already, but you can overwrite it.)
- template.php
- ajax.js
- people.json

Data File

PHP handles JSON very well, so for this example you'll store all your data in a simple JSON object. It looks a lot like regular JavaScript. Create at least six objects in the array so that you'll have enough data to do something interesting.

```
[{
    "name": "Lenny",
    "location": "Los Angeles",
    "browser": "Safari"
},
{

    "name": "Adam",
    "location": "Austin",
    "browser": "Internet Explorer"
},
// ... Add more people here
]
```

Controller File

The index.php file is a simple PHP script that manages the data and the requests from the browser, regardless of whether they're normal page requests or Ajax requests. If you don't know PHP, this script might not make a lot of sense, but you should be able to use it regardless. For the curious, the PHP Web site is a great resource: *http://us.php.net/manual/en/*. Try searching for individual functions to find reference material.

> **tip** If you run into problems writing PHP, you can use the print_r() function much like you use console.log() in JavaScript. print_r() prints a verbose description of a value to the HTML document.
>
>   print_r($people);
>
> If you're in the middle of a block of HTML, you may need to enter PHP mode like this:
>
>   <?php print_r($people); ?>

Start with this outline, and fill in the script with the code for each comment:

```php
<?php

// Reading data from the file
// Get the page number from the query string
// If there is form data, save it to the file
// Arrange the data just for this page
// If this is an ajax request, send json
// If this is a normal request, send the HTML template

?>
```

Reading Data from the File

This line loads the JSON data from the data file and stores it on a PHP variable called $people. (PHP variables always start with a dollar sign.)

```php
$people = json_decode(file_get_contents("people.json"));
if ($people == null) {
    echo "Invalid JSON file";
    exit;
}
```

Get the Page Number from the Query String

Each page should load only three people at a time, so you'll need to keep track of which page you're viewing. The $_GET variable is an array that holds query string data. The last two lines in this example keep the $page variable from being lower than zero or higher than the number of pages for the $people array.

```
$pageCount = ceil(count($people) / 3);
$page = isset($_GET["page"]) ? $_GET["page"] : 0;
$page = $page < 0 ? 0 : $page;
$page = $page >= $pageCount ? $pageCount - 1 : $page;
```

If you were to load up *http://localhost/index.php?page=2*, the $page variable would be 2.

Saving Form Data to the File

If you send form data to the page, you'll want to create a new object, add it to the $people array, and save the array to the people.json file. The $_POST variable is an array that stores form data submitted to the page. The htmlentities() function protects your HTML markup by converting characters such as < and > to encoded strings.

```
if (count($_POST)) {
    $person = new StdClass();
    $person->name = htmlentities($_POST["name"]);
    $person->location = htmlentities($_POST["location"]);
    $person->browser = htmlentities($_POST["browser"]);
    $people[] = $person;

    $fp = fopen("people.json", "w+");
    fwrite($fp, json_encode($people));
    fclose($fp);
}
```

note I'm not including any form validation to keep this example shorter. You should always validate your data before saving it to files or databases.

Arrange the Data Just for the Page

You're adding the new person object to the end of the $people array, so reverse the array to put it at the beginning. Then use the array_slice() function to extract the three person objects for the requested page.

```
$people = array_reverse($people);
$people = array_slice($people, $page * 3, 3);
```

> ## Functional vs. Object-Oriented Style
>
> The array_slice() function should look familiar: JavaScript has an analogous function that you learned about in Chapter 4. But PHP uses a functional style, where you operate on objects by passing them to functions. JavaScript uses an object-oriented style, where you act upon objects with their own methods.

Send JSON for Ajax Requests

You'll add Ajax support to index.php later in the chapter, so for now put in this somewhat useless code:

```
// Replace this with Ajax support
if (false) {
    // Ajax support goes here
```

Send an HTML Template for Normal Page Requests

When the browser requests the page normally, you want to send it a regular HTML page. Instead of putting the entire HTML markup in index.php and making it harder to read, you'll include a template file.

```
} else {
    include("template.php");
}
```

The HTML Template

The HTML document in template.php is pretty simple. It includes a table, a few navigation links, and a form.

HTML Page Outline

Start by adding this document outline to your template.php file:

```
<!DOCTYPE html>
<html>
    <head>
        <title>Ajax Test</title>
    </head>
    <body>
        <h1>Ajax Test</h1>

        <!-- Table goes here -->
        <!-- Links go here -->
        <!-- Form goes here -->

        <script src="http://ajax.googleapis.com/ajax/libs/
        ➥ jquery/1.4.1/jquery.min.js" type="text/javascript">
        ➥ </script>
        <script src="ajax.js" type="text/javascript"></script>
    </body>
</html>
```

The markup includes references to the jQuery library and the ajax.js file, which you'll create later. Replace the HTML comments with the code blocks in the following sections.

Data Table Markup

This table uses the $page and $people variables from index.php to output the data to the browser.

```
<table>
    <caption>
        People
        (Page <span id="page"><?php echo $page + 1 ?></span>)
    </caption>
    <thead>
        <tr>
            <th>Name</th>
            <th>Location</th>
            <th>Favorite Browser</th>
        </tr>
    </thead>
    <tbody>
        <?php foreach ($people as $person) : ?>
        <tr>
            <td><?php echo $person->name ?></td>
            <td><?php echo $person->location ?></td>
            <td><?php echo $person->browser ?></td>
        </tr>
        <?php endforeach; ?>
    </tbody>
</table>
```

Navigation Links

These links point back to index.php, changing the value of $page to load
a different slice of the $people array.

```
<p class="pages">
   <a href="index.php?page=<?php echo $page - 1 ?>">
   ➥ Previous</a> |
   <a href="index.php?page=<?php echo $page + 1 ?>">Next</a>
</p>
```

Form Markup

This form also points back to index.php. The method attribute is "post,"
which tells the PHP script that this form data is new data for another
person object.

```
<form action="index.php" method="post">
   <p><label for="name">Name</label><br />
   <input type="text" name="name" value="" id="name" /></p>

   <p><label for="location">Location</label><br />
   <input type="text" name="location" value=""
   ➥ id="location" /></p>

   <p><label for="browser">Favorite Browser</label><br />
   <input type="text" name="browser" value=""
   ➥ id="browser" /></p>

   <p><input type="submit" value="Submit"></p>
</form>
```

Checking Your Work

Point your browser to index.php; you should now be able to load different sets of data into the table by clicking the links, as well as add rows to
the table by submitting the form. It's great practice to start with a page
that functions perfectly well with just HTML before enhancing the experience with JavaScript and Ajax.

Ajaxifying the Page

The goal of this JavaScript file is to override the links and forms so that
the page doesn't have to refresh to load new data.

Script Outline

Here's the whole script with empty functions that you'll fill out as you
follow the example. It starts by finding the DOM elements you'll need to
add JavaScript behavior.

```
(function($) {

    var table = $("table");
    var pageLinks = $(".pages a");
    var pageCount = $("#page");
    var form = $("form");

    pageLinks.click(function(event) {});
    function loadingFunc() {}
    function errorFunc() {}
    function successFunc(response) {}
    function insertJson(people) {}
    function templatize(template, obj) {}
    function updatePageLinks(pageNum) {}        (continues on next page)
```

```
    form.submit(function(event) {});
```

```
})(jQuery); // Self-invoking function executes automatically
```

Overriding the Previous and Next Links

The navigation links should get event handlers that do two important things:

- Stop the browser from following the link by preventing the default behavior

- Load the link's target (its href attribute value) with Ajax instead

```
pageLinks.click(function(event) {
    event.preventDefault();

    $.ajax({
        url : $(this).attr("href"),
        beforeSend : loadingFunc,
        error : errorFunc,
        success : successFunc
    });
});
```

jQuery's $.ajax() function takes an object as an argument. That object can have numerous properties (see *http://api.jquery.com/jQuery.ajax/* for details). For this script, you're mostly concerned with setting functions to handle various stages of the Ajax request.

Waiting for the Request to Load

The loadingFunc() function adds a message to the <caption> element that tells the user that something is happening. The message displays

"Loading …" until the Ajax request finishes (\u2026 is the Unicode escape sequence for an ellipsis).

```
function loadingFunc() {
   var message = $("<div/>", {
      className : "message"
   }).text("Loading \u2026");
   table.find("caption").append(message);
}
```

Error Handling

If the user were to point the browser to a missing page, it would show them an error message. If an Ajax request fails, the browser doesn't inform the user, so you'll have to do it for them. The errorFunc() function changes the "Loading …" message to an error message.

```
function errorFunc() {
   $(".message").text("Error loading data.");
}
```

Handling the Response

The last Ajax callback function handles a successful response and updates the page accordingly.

```
function successFunc(response) {
   table.find(".message").remove();
   insertJson(response.people);
   updatePageLinks(+response.page); // Convert string to
   ➡ number with +
}
```

You still need to update index.php to handle an Ajax response before this will work. Replace the if (false) statement in index.php with the following code:

```
if ($_SERVER["HTTP_X_REQUESTED_WITH"] == "XMLHttpRequest") {
    sleep(1);
    header("Content-type: application/json");
    $response = new StdClass();
    $response->page = $page;
    $response->people = $people;
    echo json_encode($response);
} else {
    include("template.php");
}
```

jQuery sets a *request header* called X_REQUESTED_WITH to "XMLHttpRequest." That's how you can differentiate between normal page requests and Ajax requests. (This does *not* happen automatically with Ajax or with other JavaScript libraries.)

The sleep() function adds an artificial delay; without it, you probably wouldn't be able to see the "Loading ..." message.

The header() function sets a *response header* that indicates the data format of the response. jQuery handles application/json responses as JSON. (This also doesn't happen automatically with Ajax or other JavaScript libraries.)

Lastly, the $response object contains two pieces of information: the current page number and the $people array. The echo keyword outputs the JSON response, which looks similar to the following:

```
{
    "page" : 1,
```

```
    "people" : [
        // People objects
    ]
}
```

The Firebug console displays Ajax requests, so at this point you can make sure everything works by loading index.php in the browser and clicking Next (**Figure 15.1**). Now that you can request data over Ajax, the next step is to present the data to the user by updating the page.

Figure 15.1
Firebug lets you inspect the Ajax request and response.

Updating the User Interface

The insertJson() function loops over all the people objects from the JSON response and creates HTML strings using a template. Once it creates <tr> elements for each person object, it empties the table and inserts the new HTML into the page.

```
function insertJson(people) {
    var template = "<tr><td>{name}</td><td>{location}</td>
    ➥ <td>{browser}</td></tr>";
    var results = [];

    for (var i = 0, l = people.length; i < l; i++) {
        results.push(templatize(template, people[i]));
    }                                           (continues on next page)
```

```
      return table.find("tbody").empty().append(results.
      ➥ join("\n"));
}

function templatize(template, obj) {
      return template.replace(/\{([^\}]+)\}/g,
      ➥ function(match, subpattern) {
            return obj[subpattern] == null ? "" : obj[subpattern];
      });
}
```

note The templatize() function is a sophisticated usage of regular expressions and the replace() method that maps words inside curly braces (such as "{name}") with the property names of an object.

The updatePageLinks() function changes the <caption> and the navigation links to reflect the new page loaded in with Ajax. The href attributes of the "Previous" and "Next" links change to point to pageNum - 1 and pageNum + 1, respectively.

```
function updatePageLinks(pageNum) {
      pageCount.text(pageNum + 1);
      var pattern = /\bpage=\-?\d+/;
      pageLinks.eq(0).attr("href", function(index, value) {
            return value.replace(pattern, "page=" + (pageNum - 1));
      });
      pageLinks.eq(1).attr("href", function(index, value) {
            return value.replace(pattern, "page=" + (pageNum + 1));
      });
}
```

At this point, the Previous and Next links should work without reloading the page.

Overriding the Form

Adding a submit event handler to the `<form>` is the final step. It's almost exactly the same as the navigation link handler.

```
form.submit(function(event) {
    event.preventDefault();

    $.ajax({
        url : form.attr("action"),
        type : form.attr("method"),
        data : form.serialize(),
        beforeSend : loadingFunc,
        error : errorFunc,
        success : successFunc
    });
});
```

The differences make this Ajax request send POST data to index.php in an Ajax request. The type property comes from the method attribute of the form (which is "post"). The value of the data attribute uses the jQuery serialize() method to turn all the form inputs into an object.

This is definitely one of the most complicated examples in this book because of the complex interactions between the server PHP code and browser JavaScript code. If you made it through without too many hiccups, pat yourself on the back—you're well on your way toward being a JavaScript master.

Getting Around the Same-Origin Policy

One of the most popular uses for JavaScript is the creation of mash-ups, pulling data from different sites and combining it in useful and interesting ways. The same-origin policy, while being an important security restriction, makes this more difficult than it should be. Here are a few ways to circumvent the policy.

Proxies

You can set up a script on your own server that redirects an Ajax request to another server, taking advantage of the flexibility of server-to-server communication. Try searching the Web for some example scripts.

JSON-P

You can't request data from another server with Ajax, but you can load JavaScript from another server with <script> tags. JSON with Padding (JSON-P) takes advantage of this fact. Here's a quick example that loads data from Twitter:

```
<script type="text/javascript">
    function twitterCallback(tweets) {
        alert("Latest Tweet: " + tweets[0].text);
    }
</script>
<script src="http://twitter.com/status/user_timeline/
➥ whitehouse.json?callback=twitterCallback" type="text/
➥ javascript"></script>
```

The first <script> defines a function called twitterCallback() that
consumes the Twitter JavaScript data. The second <script> loads a
special JavaScript file using the Twitter API, passing the name of the
twitterCallback() as a parameter. The Twitter JavaScript file looks like
the following:

```
twitterCallback([{
   "user": {
      "screen_name": "whitehouse",
   },
   "text": "\"Feeling the Olympic Spirit\": Valerie Jarrett
   ➥ reports back from Vancouver, with photos http://bit.ly/
   ➥ aGibb1"
},
// ... More tweets
]);
```

The JavaScript file immediately executes the callback function and
delivers the data as an argument. You can dynamically create <script>
tags at any point in your code to request data from other servers with
JSON-P APIs.

note   JSON-P is inherently less secure than sending data with Ajax, so don't
        use it with passwords and other sensitive information.

16

Animation

Animation is actually a pretty simple concept. At its most basic, animation is just the process of changing a value over time. That value could be the position, size, opacity, or even color of an HTML element. Used appropriately, JavaScript animation can help create a dynamic and engaging user experience for your Web site.

Animation has endless uses, so instead of a specific example, I'll show you how to program animation utilities from the ground up. It's also a great example of asynchronous programming and the global timer functions from Chapter 7.

Simple Animation

The following examples use this HTML document, which simply draws a small black box, to demonstrate animation concepts:

```
<!DOCTYPE html>
<html>
   <head>
      <title>Animation</title>
      <style type="text/css" media="screen">
         #box {
            background: #000;
            width: 25px;
            height: 25px;
            position: absolute;
            left: 0;
            top: 0;
         }
      </style>
   </head>
   <body>
      <div id="box"></div>
      <script type="text/javascript">
         // Animation code goes here
      </script>
   </body>
</html>
```

The simplest animation involves changing a property by a little bit every interval of time. For example, this function moves an element to the left from 0 to 100, by adding one every ten milliseconds:

```
function simpleAnimation(box) {
    var position = 0;

    function move() {
        position++; // Move by 1
        if (position < 100) {
            box.style.left = position + "px";
            // Call move() again after 10 ms
            setTimeout(move, 10);
        }
    }
    move(); // Start the animation
}
simpleAnimation(document.getElementById("box"));
```

The inner function, move(), calls itself repeatedly with a ten-millisecond delay using setTimeout(). The position variable increments and updates the box's style.left property until it equals 100, when the animation stops.

However, this animation pattern has limited use. More frequently, you'll want to specify a duration and let the animation function figure out how to increment the value each interval.

Time-Based Animation

The general idea behind time-based animation is tricky to explain, but it's actually pretty simple. There's a direct relationship between the distance traveled and the time passed since starting the animation.

```javascript
function timeBased(box, begin, end, duration) {
    var distanceToTravel = end - begin,
        startTime = new Date().getTime();

    function move() {
        // A number in milliseconds
        var timePassed = new Date().getTime() - startTime;
        // A number between 0 to 1
        var percentPassed = timePassed / duration;

        if (timePassed < duration) {
            var newValue = (distanceToTravel *
            ➡ percentPassed) + begin;
            box.style.left = newValue + "px";
            setTimeout(move, 0);
        } else {
            box.style.left = end + "px";
        }
    }
    move(); // Start the animation
}
timeBased(document.getElementById("box"), 0, 200, 1000);
```

The first thing timeBased() does is calculate how far to travel, or the end value minus the begin value. Second, it stores the current time so you can easily tell how much time has passed on the next interval.

Like in the simpleAnimation() function, the inner move() function calls itself repeatedly with setTimeout(). This time, the interval is zero milliseconds (which really means "as soon as possible"). The smaller the delay, the smoother the animation.

The first thing move() does is calculate how much time has passed since startTime. That value is in milliseconds, but to turn time into distance, you want a simple percentage of how much time has passed. By dividing timePassed by the desired duration, you get a number between 0 and 1. At 0, the animation has just begun. At 1, the animation is complete. And at 0.5, the animation is halfway done.

If the amount of time passed is less than the duration, then move() updates the style.left property according to this formula:

(Distance to travel * Percentage of duration passed) + Beginning value

You might remember this as $y = mx+b$, or a linear algebraic equation.

If the duration of time has passed, then move() just sets style.left to the ending value and does not repeat itself.

Time-based animation has three main benefits:

- It's easier to keep animations in sync because you know exactly how long they are going to take.

- If the browser gets tied up with another process, the animation might stutter a bit but will still complete in the desired duration.

- You're not limited to linear animations, as you'll see in a moment.

The Date Data Type

I haven't discussed the Date data type yet, but it's one of the built-in data types like String and Function. Here are a few example uses of the Date data type:

```
// Create a date object for the current time
var date = new Date();
date;
Sun Feb 15 2010 19:01:26 GMT-0800 (PST) {}

// Create a date object specifying a certain time
// year, month, day, hours, minutes, seconds, ms
// January is 0, February is 1
var mayanApocalypse = new Date(2012, 0, 1, 0, 0, 0, 0);
mayanApocalypse;
Sun Jan 01 2012 00:00:00 GMT-0800 (PST) {}

// Get the millisecond representation of a date.
// This is useful for comparing dates
mayanApocalypse.getTime();
1325404800000

// Getting and setting various parts of the date
date.setDate(date.getDate() + 1); // tomorrow
1266376009093
date.getMonth();
1
```

Easing

Easing refers to using curved equations for more graceful or expressive animation. There are three basic types:

- *Ease out* is when the animation gradually slows as it ends.
- *Ease in* is when the animation gradually speeds up as it starts.
- *Ease in/out* is a combination of both.

First rewrite the timeBased() function to use easing equations. I usually shorten some variable names to match the equations: t is timePassed, c is distanceToTravel (or "change"), b is begin, e is end, and d is duration.

```
function timeBasedEasing(box, b, e, d, easing) {
   var c = e - b,
      startTime = new Date();

   function move() {
      var t = new Date() - startTime;

      if (t < d) {
         box.style.left = easing(t, b, c, d) + "px";
         setTimeout(move, 0);
      } else {
         box.style.left = e + "px";
      }
   }
   move(); // Start the animation
}
```

The function is basically identical to timeBased(), except that it offloads most of the calculation to the easing argument. Next, create the linear easing equation:

```
function linear(t, b, c, d) {
    return c*t/d + b;
}
```

note The easing functions in this chapter come from Robert Penner's Easing Equations for ActionScript, released under a BSD License: *http://www.robertpenner.com/easing_terms_of_use.html*.

Then, you can call the timeBasedEasing() function with the linear() function as an argument:

```
timeBasedEasing(document.getElementById("box"), 0, 200, 1000,
➥ linear);
```

There's nothing surprising there, but you can swap linear() with a function like this:

```
function easeOutExpo(t, b, c, d) {
    return (t==d) ? b+c : c * (-Math.pow(2, -10 * t/d) + 1) + b;
}
timeBasedEasing(document.getElementById("box"), 0, 200, 1000,
➥ easeOutExpo);
```

The animation starts much faster and "eases" to a stop. The "ease in" version looks like this:

```
function easeInExpo(t, b, c, d) {
    return (t==0) ? b : c * Math.pow(2, 10 * (t/d - 1)) + b;
}
timeBasedEasing(document.getElementById("box"), 0, 200, 1000,
➥ easeInExpo);
```

There are even more easing functions for elastic and bouncing movement, but they're too complicated to include in this book.

Check out Robert Penner's library of ActionScript equations at *http://www.robertpenner.com/easing/*. ActionScript is another dialect of ECMAScript, so the equations are easily translated to JavaScript.

Animation with Libraries

Animation is a pretty simple concept, but it's still a lot easier to use a JavaScript library to create animation utilities than writing them from scratch. Library animation utilities allow you to do many things:

- Set the ending values for multiple properties at once

- Set the duration and easing equations

- Add callback functions that trigger at the end of the animation

To see how both the YUI 3 and jQuery libraries handle this, replace the <script> element in the previous example HTML with the following markup:

```
<p><a href="#" id="yuiLink">Animate with YUI</a></p>
<p><a href="#" id="jqueryLink">Animate with jQuery</a></p>
<p><a href="#" id="reset">Reset</a></p>

<script src="http://yui.yahooapis.com/3.0.0/build/yui/
➥yui-min.js" type="text/javascript"></script>
<script src="http://ajax.googleapis.com/ajax/libs/jquery/
➥1.4.1/jquery.min.js" type="text/javascript"></script>
<script src="animation.js" type="text/javascript"></script>
```

note   **There's really no reason to load two libraries into a page at once, but at least YUI 3 and jQuery play nicely with each other by using namespacing and closures to encapsulate their code.**

YUI 3 Animation Objects

In a new file, animation.js, add the following code to create a YUI 3 animation object:

```
YUI().use("anim", function(Y) {

    var animation = new Y.Anim({
        node: "#box",
        to: {
            width: 200,
            height: 100,
            left: 50,
            top: 150,
            backgroundColor: "#f00"
        },
        duration: 2, // In seconds
        easing: Y.Easing.easeOut
    });

    // Continue YUI 3 code here

});
```

The Y.Anim constructor function creates an object you can control later in the script. The node parameter takes a selector like the one you would pass to Y.one() to select a single DOM element. You can find the rest of the parameters in the online documentation: *http://developer.yahoo.com/yui/3/api/Anim.html#configattributes*.

Continuing the YUI 3 version of the script, you can add an event handler to the animation object that fires when the animation ends:

```
animation.on("end", animationCallback);
```

Add this callback function *outside* the YUI closure function so you can use it in the jQuery example too:

```
function animationCallback() {
    console.log("animation finished!");
}
```

The code so far doesn't actually start the execution. Add an event handler to the first <a> element in the page:

```
// Inside the YUI closure function
Y.one("#yuiLink").on("click", function(event) {
    event.preventDefault();
    animation.run();
});
```

The run() method starts the animation, and after two seconds, the callback function will print "animation finished!" to the console.

The jQuery animate() Method

jQuery takes a slightly different approach to animation and has a slightly different set of capabilities. Create a second closure function in animation.js for the following jQuery code:

```
(function($) {

    $("#jqueryLink").click(function(event) {
        event.preventDefault();

        $("#box").animate({
            width: 200,
            height: 100,
            left: 50,
```

(continues on next page)

```
        top: 150
    }, {
        duration: 2000, // In ms
        complete: animationCallback
    });
  });

})(jQuery);
```

The `animate()` method runs immediately instead of returning an object to control later. It can take several combinations of arguments; the online documentation at *http://api.jquery.com/animate/* covers all the variations. In this example, the first argument specifies the ending values for the properties you want to animate. The second argument specifies parameters such as the duration and any callback functions.

Other difference between YUI 3 and jQuery in terms of animation include the following:

- You can animate only a single object with a YUI 3 single Y.Anim object, whereas jQuery's `animate()` function can animate multiple elements at once in one method call.

- YUI 3 includes a number of easing functions automatically, which you can find here: *http://developer.yahoo.com/yui/3/api/Easing.html*. jQuery includes only two easing functions by default, "linear" and "swing."

- jQuery can't animate color values by default. The jQuery UI library adds this capability, as well as additional easing equations.

Resetting Animation

Animations work by changing the `style` attribute, so you can reset the animation by setting the attribute to an empty string. This is one case where you have to use the setAttribute() method, because the style property is read-only.

```
document.getElementById("box").style = "";
TypeError: setting a property that has only a getter
document.getElementById("box").setAttribute("style", "");
```

You can add an event handler for the Reset link using either YUI 3 or jQuery. Here's the YUI 3 version:

```
Y.one("#reset").on("click", function(event) {
    event.preventDefault();
    Y.one("#box").setAttribute("style", "");
});
```

Using Animation

You have a lot of freedom when animating DOM elements. I tend to follow a couple simple rules when using animation on my sites:

- Easing equations, especially exponential equations, make animations feel more natural and expressive.

- Animations should ideally enhance the usability of the user interface. For example, a quick flip between two elements might be easy to miss, but a slow transition can tell the user where the new content comes from.

- Subtlety is key. If you have too many elements moving around the page, you'll distract the user from your content.

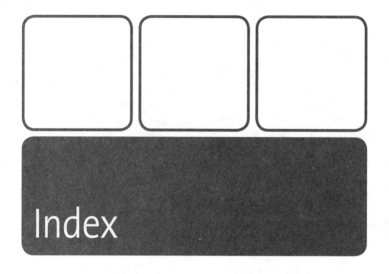

Index